D1685646

an de Montfort

erative Education

Pierre Juan de Montfort

A Model of Co-operative Education

on Peace Support Operations in Africa

LAP LAMBERT Academic Publishing

Impressum/Imprint (nur für Deutschland/ only for Germany)
Bibliografische Information der Deutschen Nationalbibliothek: Die Deutsche Nationalbibliothek verzeichnet diese Publikation in der Deutschen Nationalbibliografie; detaillierte bibliografische Daten sind im Internet über http://dnb.d-nb.de abrufbar.
Alle in diesem Buch genannten Marken und Produktnamen unterliegen warenzeichen-, marken- oder patentrechtlichem Schutz bzw. sind Warenzeichen oder eingetragene Warenzeichen der jeweiligen Inhaber. Die Wiedergabe von Marken, Produktnamen, Gebrauchsnamen, Handelsnamen, Warenbezeichnungen u.s.w. in diesem Werk berechtigt auch ohne besondere Kennzeichnung nicht zu der Annahme, dass solche Namen im Sinne der Warenzeichen- und Markenschutzgesetzgebung als frei zu betrachten wären und daher von jedermann benutzt werden dürften.

Coverbild: www.ingimage.com

Verlag: LAP LAMBERT Academic Publishing AG & Co. KG
Dudweiler Landstr. 99, 66123 Saarbrücken, Deutschland
Telefon +49 681 3720-310, Telefax +49 681 3720-3109
Email: info@lap-publishing.com

Herstellung in Deutschland:
Schaltungsdienst Lange o.H.G., Berlin
Books on Demand GmbH, Norderstedt
Reha GmbH, Saarbrücken
Amazon Distribution GmbH, Leipzig
ISBN: 978-3-8383-0127-3

Imprint (only for USA, GB)
Bibliographic information published by the Deutsche Nationalbibliothek: The Deutsche Nationalbibliothek lists this publication in the Deutsche Nationalbibliografie; detailed bibliographic data are available in the Internet at http://dnb.d-nb.de.
Any brand names and product names mentioned in this book are subject to trademark, brand or patent protection and are trademarks or registered trademarks of their respective holders. The use of brand names, product names, common names, trade names, product descriptions etc. even without a particular marking in this works is in no way to be construed to mean that such names may be regarded as unrestricted in respect of trademark and brand protection legislation and could thus be used by anyone.

Cover image: www.ingimage.com

Publisher: LAP LAMBERT Academic Publishing AG & Co. KG
Dudweiler Landstr. 99, 66123 Saarbrücken, Germany
Phone +49 681 3720-310, Fax +49 681 3720-3109
Email: info@lap-publishing.com

Printed in the U.S.A.
Printed in the U.K. by (see last page)
ISBN: 978-3-8383-0127-3

Central University of
Technology, Free State

A MODEL OF CO-OPERATIVE EDUCATION ON
PEACE SUPPORT OPERATIONS IN AFRICA

LT COL PIERRE JUAN DE MONTFORT

TABLE OF CONTENTS

CHAPTER 3: RESEARCH DESIGN AND METHODOLOGY

CHAPTER 4: RESEARCH RESULTS

CHAPTER 5: FINDINGS AND RECOMMENDATIONS

LIST OF FIGURES

LIST OF TABLES

LIST OF ACRONYMS

AC – Abstract conceptualisation

ADDIE - Analysis, Design, Development, Implement, Evaluate

AE – Active experimentation

AIDS – Acquired Immune Deficiency Syndrome

ASF – African Standby Force

AU – African Union

AWOL – Absence without official leave

C2 - Command and Control

CA - Civil Affairs

CAI - Computer Assisted Instruction

CE – Concrete experience

CIMIC - Civil-Military Coordination Process

CIVPOL – Civilian Police

COE - Contingent-Owned Equipment

COLET – College of Education Technology

CUT – Central University of Technology, Free State

CRI - Criterion Referenced Instruction

CRP – Command Research Paper

DDR - Disarmament, Demobilisation, and Reintegration

DOD – Department of Defence

DRC - Democratic Republic of the Congo

ECOWAS - Economic Community of West African States

ED Tech – Educational Technology

EOD - Explosive Ordnance Disposal

ELO – Exit Level Outcome

ETD – Education Training and Development

ETDP – Education Training and Development Practitioner

ETQA – Education Training Qualifications Authority

G8 – Group of Eight Countries

GPCT – General Purpose Combat Training

GEO-POL – Geographical and Political Studies

HA - Humanitarian Assistance

HIV – Human Immunodeficiency Virus

HQ – Headquarters

HR – Human Resources

ICRC - International Committee of the Red Cross

IDP – Internally displaced people

IED - Improvised Explosive Device

IFOR - Implementation Force

IHL - International Humanitarian Law

IO – International Organisation

IOM - International Organisation for Migration

IMPI - Indigenous Military Peace-building Initiative

IMAS - International Mine Action Standards

IRC – International Red Cross

ISD – Instructional Design

ISS – Institute for Strategic Studies

JA - Yugoslav Army

JSCSP - Joint Senior Command and Staff Programme

KLA - Kosovo Liberation Army

KSA – Knowledge, Skills and Attributes

LOAC - Law of Armed Conflict

MBT – Mine Ban Treaty

MILOBS – UN Military Observer

MILOPS – Military Operations

MSCA - Military Support to Civil Authorities

MOOTW - Military Operations other than War

MONUC - UN mission in the Democratic Republic of the Congo

MP – Member of Parliament

NATO - North Atlantic Treaty Organisation

NCO – Non-commissioned Officer

NEO - Non-combatant Evacuation Operations

NEPAD - New Partnership for Africa's Development

NGO – Non-governmental Organisation

NIHE - Northern Cape Institute for Higher Learning

NQF – National Qualifications Framework

NRF – National Research Foundation

OBE – Outcomes Based Education

OSCE - Organisation of Security Co-operation in Europe

ONUSAL - The United Nations Observer Mission in El Salvador

ONUMOZ - The United Nations Operation in Mozambique

PBT - Performance-Based Training

PCM - Project Cycle Management

PDA - Plan, Develop, and Assess

PE – Peace enforcement

PfP - African Partnership for Peace

PK - Peacekeeping

PSO – Peace Support Operations

PTSD - Post-Traumatic Stress Disorder

PO – Peace Operations

POW - Prisoners of War

PVO – Private Voluntary Organisation

SA Army - South African Army

SAHMS - The SA Medical Health Services

SADC – Southern African Development Community

SANDF – South African National Defence Force

SANWC - South African National War College

SAARDHE - South African Association for Research Development

SAQA – South Africa Qualifications Authority

SAT - Systems Approach to Training

SASCE - South African Association for Co-operative Education

SEBO – School for Entrepreneurship and Business Development

SFOR - Stabilization Force

SSR – Security Sector Reform

STDs - Sexually Transmitted Diseases

TB – Tuberculosis

TCC – Troop Contributing Country

TEWT - Tactical Exercise without Troops

TUT – Tswane University of Technology

RDP - Reconstruction and Development Program

RO – Reflective observation

RSA – Republic of South Africa

RPD - Rapid Prototyping Design

RPL – Recognition of prior learning

UN – United Nations

UNEF - UN Emergency Force

UNISA - University of South Africa

UNTAG - United Nations Transition Assistance Group

UNTAC - The United Nations Transitional Authority in Cambodia

ONUC - UN Operation in the Congo

UNHCR - UN High Commission for Refugees

UNICEF - UN Children's Fund

UNFICYP - UN Peacekeeping force in Cyprus

UNIFIL - UN interim force in Lebanon

UNITAR POCI – United Nations Institute for Training and Research Peacekeeping Operations Correspondence Instruction

UNOSOM I - The First United Nations Operation in Somalia

UNPROFOR - The United Nations Protection Force in the Former Yugoslavia

UK – United Kingdom

USA – United States of America

UXO - Unexploded Ordnance

WACE - World Association for Co-Operative Education

WFP – World Food Programme

WHO – World Health Organisation

WO – Warrant Officer

SYNOPSIS

The focus of this study is on a Model of Co-operative Education on Peace Support Operations (PSO) in Africa.

PSO are multi-functional operations involving military forces and diplomatic humanitarian agencies. They are designed to achieve humanitarian goals or a long-term political settlement, and are conducted impartially in support of a UN mandate. These include peacekeeping (PK), peace enforcement (PE), conflict prevention, peacemaking, peace building, and humanitarian operations.

Since the advent of democracy in 1994, domestic and international expectations have steadily grown regarding a new South African role as a responsible and respected member of the international community. These expectations have included a hope that South Africa will play a leading role in a variety of international, regional and sub-regional forums, and that the country will become an active participant in attempts to resolve various regional and international conflicts.

Peacekeeping is becoming more and more important as South Africa plays a vital role in African missions, mandates, deployment and restructuring. The core of peacekeeping operations in Africa is no longer about the deployment of armed forces, but the focus is shifting towards a more integrated approach including reconstruction, development, stability, civilian involvement and humanitarian aspects. While skills required for peace operations overlap with those required for war, there is increasing recognition that additional peace operations training is needed to successfully conduct these missions.

The demand, advancement and application of peacekeeping evolve worldwide, especially in Africa, where enormous funding is being poured into local research and development, testing and training.

The market for Education, Training and Development (ETD) in the field of PSO is growing, as South Africa is becoming increasingly involved in peacekeeping missions on the African continent. At present, there is no Co-operative Education programme on generic PSO on the operational/strategic level presented by any of the major universities in South Africa in order to enhance other PSO training.

The principal product (output) of this research will consist out of an ISD report on a Model for Co-operative Education on PSO in Africa, presented by means of Correspondence Instruction with contact sessions. The key factors in production of the learning program include geo-political and security studies in order to create an understanding of the African battle space, PSO as presented by UNITAR POCI, the assessment of international practice with regards to PSO in order to relate the information to operations in Africa, PSO on the African continent, and Civil-Military Cooperation.

CHAPTER 1 - INTRODUCTION

1.1   **BACKGROUND**

The primary purpose of the United Nations (UN) is to maintain international peace and security (UN Department of Peacekeeping Operations, 1995:3), and to end the "scourge of war" (Charter of the UN: 1945). According to Deen (2006:5) UN peacekeeping operations have become an indispensable weapon in the arsenal of the international community and there is growing confidence in UN peacekeeping as a means to help build stability after conflict.

Throughout the duration of the Cold War, UN peace support operations (PSO) were constrained by superpower rivalry and remained relatively small. Despite more than 80 wars fought world wide (James, 1990), only 13 UN peacekeeping and observer missions were conducted between 1948 and 1988 (Roberts, 1996). After the Cold War, the number of UN peacekeeping or observer forces increased and, at the end of 1994, these missions were staffed by 77,783 civilian (Boutros-Ghali, 1996:4) and military personnel from over 82 different nations, serving on 19 missions (Liu, 1999:8). Now in 2006 the UN has recorded a historic high of 80, 976 soldiers and 15,000 civilian peacekeepers from 112 countries and is set to total 140,000 by 2007 (Deen, 2006:5).

The current trends of political, social, and economic globalisation has resulted in an increase in the number of conflicts, aggravated by instability, social and economic injustice, and political competition (Hårleman, 2003: 8).

17

The UN is confronted with a significant change in the nature of conflict. Instead of wars in which two nations with professional armies face each other, today's conflict is typically an internal struggle with irregular forces, light weapons and guerrilla tactics. There are not merely two opposing forces, but include rival warlords, factional leaders, para-military forces and even organised criminal groups (Standard Generic Training Module, 2003: 3-4).

These so-called 'third generation' operations are triggered by the resurgence of suppressed and very old animosity. Conflicts are characterised by abuses of human rights. Moreover, consent may be absent, since authority has collapsed and is meaningless because of a large number of groups claiming power. Agreements are non-existent or worthless and international law and conventions are openly disobeyed (Malan 1996:3).

In this environment, UN peacekeeping has become increasingly complex and multi-dimensional, requiring a variety of civilian, police and military actors (Higate, 2004:3). It is therefore essential that training is available to familiarize personnel with established doctrine. Such training must be standard, doctrinally correct, and easily delivered.

1.2   RATIONALE FOR THE RESEARCH

The security of Africa has deteriorated since 1989, when the Cold War ended. Insurgents often gain power and some states involve themselves militarily in their neighbour's affairs. Diminished foreign interest, a change in the nature of African conflicts and personal dictatorial rule in many African states have been the main causes of deterioration. Many African wars are rooted in ethnic quarrel (Kruys, 2004:35).

In addition, the end of the Cold War reduced the military-strategic importance of Africa in world politics and increased claims for democracy encouraged civil conflict in various African nations.

A high proportion of youth, rapid urban growth, low levels of cropland and excessive adult mortality, mostly due to high HIV and AIDS prevalence, are further factors increasing risks levels for civil conflict (Cincotta, Engelman and Anastasion, 2003:13).

Africa has emerged as a dangerous and challenging environment for the conduct of contemporary peace operations (Potgieter, 1996:1). The challenges and constraints of peacekeeping in African countries such as Somalia and Rwanda led to unwillingness by the major powers to become involved in peacekeeping efforts in Africa (Neethling, 1999:22-23). At the start of the 21st century Africa is unstable and rent by wars leading to famine, brutality, disease and failing economies (Kruys, 2004;15). There exists no doubt that Africa is brimming with poverty and underdevelopment. Africa has the lowest per capita income in the world (Daniels, 2005:4).

This state of affairs led to calls made by President Thabo Mbeki for an Africa-renaissance that amounts to Africans accepting responsibility for their own destiny (Steyn, 1997:12) and accountability for conflict prevention and resolution on the continent through co-operation at regional and sub-regional level (Thiart, 1997:12). Nelson Mandela put forward the national value: "South Africa cannot escape its African destiny" (Mandela, 1993).

Corresponding to calls for a renaissance the New Partnership for Africa's Development (NEPAD) is arguable the most important socio-economic plan ever to emerge from Africa - an 'African solution to African problems.' The programme links aid to good governance and set preconditions for its success to include peace and security (Ramsbotham, Bah and Calder, 2005:2).

If NEPAD is to be viable, the role of African militaries will have to be acknowledged and defined (Engelbrecht, 2002:22). In reaction, the African Union (AU) proposed the establishment of an African Standby Force (ASF) and the G8 countries have pledged assistance to African peacekeeping efforts as part of their Africa action plan to support NEPAD (Fabricius, 2003:11).

South Africa has declared itself willing to contribute to PSO under the auspices of the UN, the AU and Southern African development Community (SADC) (Kent and Malan: 2003:1). The White Paper on Defence (1996:20) acknowledges the expectation for South Africa to participate in PSO. The Defence Review (1998:36) stipulates that the South African National Defence Force (SANDF) may become involved in PSO as part of a multinational peace force. The White Paper on Participation in International Peacekeeping Operations (1998:2) states that South Africa's potential contributions may include the voluntary services of a diverse group of civilians.

In January 2001, President Thabo Mbeki told the world economic forum at Davos that the key priority for Africa was creating peace, security, stability, and democratic governance, as without which it would be impossible to engage in meaningful economic activity. South African Defence Minister Mosiuoa Lekota concurs that there will be no development without security (Heitman, 2005b:21).

In an interview with Helmoed-Römer Heitman (2005a:34) the Chief of the South African (SA) Army, Lt Gen Solly Shoke, said, "It's our duty to participate in PSOs."

Judging from the statements the Republic of South Africa (RSA) will remain involved in PSO in Africa for political, economic and moral reasons to help resolve conflicts on the continent, since ignoring them could mean instability that would impinge on South Africa economically and otherwise. Conflict, instability and a lack of security in Africa have been the key factors both in frightening off investment and in making self-funded economic development difficult (Morris, 2003:12).

The core of PSO in Africa does no longer merely entail the deployment of armed forces, but the focus is on shifting towards a more integrated approach including reconstruction, development, stability, civilian involvement and humanitarian aspects (International Quality and Productivity Centre: 2006).

Since 2000, SANDF soldiers have been deploying on the continent for peacekeeping missions (Tsedu, 2002:6). Jankielsohn (2003:21), a member of parliament, urges government to acknowledge that the SANDF has a limited capacity to deploy troops in PSO over long periods. It has neither the logistical nor the personnel capacity to do so. The SANDF has health problems arising from a 21% HIV/AIDS infection rate (Katzenellenbogen, 2004:3). According to Boshoff (Financial Mail, 2004:25) SANDF resources have stretched to the limit by its peacekeeping obligations, prompting a review of current policy.

An index published in the International Security Review is of the opinion that South Africa's military potency is slipping (Trench, 1998:15). According to Heitman (2003:12), an army lives and dies literally by its training. Soldiers, units and formations must train frequently, regularly and thoroughly for an army to be effective. Any slippage in the training programme will eventually result in casualties.

Linking to this, one of the areas of greatest concern in South Africa is the extremely low level of education of the majority of the population (Jerling, 1999:12). More than 75% of the South African labour force is functionally illiterate in the sense that they do not have the skills that are required to perform most job tasks effectively and efficiently (Ernst, 2000:1). According to Harrison (1989:12), education directly and indirectly affects the development of knowledge and skills. Invariably, only people who are educated, trained and developed can be productive and contribute significantly (Erasmus and van Dyk, 1999: 15).

In an environment of rapid change, Education, Training and Development (ETD), has become the driving force for meeting the demand for skilled workers to manage the new social and economic challenges (Van Dyk, Nel, Loedolff and Haasbroek, 2001:5). Van der Westhuizen (1998:34) agrees by stating that countries and organisations will only be able to cope with a fast changing world if they adopt an innovative approach to ETD.

Allen (1998:2) says that training is fundamental in becoming more productive. As a result, to succeed the SANDF, other government and non-government organisations (NGOs) involved in PSO have no other alternative but to properly educate, train and develop its people (SA White Paper on Defence, 1996:10).

By using ETD as force multiplier, the SANDF will be able to meet future force demands (Van der Westhuizen, 1998:11), and create learning conditions to prepare South Africans to meet the demands of globalisation (Brown and Brown, 1994:3-39).

1.3 **STATEMENT OF PROBLEM**

The awareness of a problem base on the perception that not everything is as it should be (Wolmarans and Eksteen, 1987:8). There is a need for conceptual clarity on principles of doctrine for the conduct of increasingly complex peace operations - especially those where there are parties bent on using violence to derail the peace process.

Programs such as those of the UN Institute for Training and Research Peacekeeping Operations Correspondence Instruction (UNITA POCI) and Co-operative Education are important to help bridge the illiteracy gap. However, it is also important that the African doctrine for PSO not only derive from abroad. African realities should inform military operations (MILOPS) that are inevitably different from the environment that has shaped European and American doctrinal development (Training for Peace, 2004:1).

The researcher knows from experience that, in preparing its forces for peace support missions, the SA Army relies almost exclusively on a core of general-purpose combat training, supplemented by mission-specific training during the pre-conflict phase. The reliance on general-purpose combat training base on the conviction that troops well trained for high-intensity warfare would be well prepared for any scenario falling short of combat, including peacekeeping. It assumes that peacekeeping draws on the same set of skills as conventional warfare, but tests soldiers to a lesser degree and that any necessary training beyond general-purpose combat training is achievable within the relatively short period between the notice of mission and a unit's actual deployment.

Regrettably, this traditional approach to training is not adequate to give military personnel either the full range of skills or the appropriate orientation necessary to meet the diverse and complex challenges presented in African peace support operations. The topics relevant to training for PSO are many and complex and could possibly not be covered adequately in the pre-conflict phase, particularly in cases where that period measure in days. The failure of the formal training plan to provide satisfactorily for these non-combat skills arise primarily from the lack of doctrine recognising the need for such training and the lack of supporting training materials and standards.

According to Malan, (1996:11) doctrinal elasticity and attempts to train soldiers "across the spectrum of conflict from stability operations to war," must be avoided, for they imply a complex and confusing mix of the use of armed force on the one hand, with concepts such as neutrality, impartiality and the minimum use of necessary force on the other.

Southern Africa simply lacks the foundational capacity to create forces that are ubiquitous and capable of discharging tasks across the spectrum of 'peace operation' roles. A more realistic vision would be the creation of a readily available, multilateral pool of competent peacekeepers at the regional or sub-regional level to prevent the reigniting of conflict and the creation of a separate, effective and rapidly deployable multilateral enforcement formation able to stop conflict before it gets serious.

Van Dyk et al. (2001:175) differentiate between three types of problems: managerial, systems and performance. The absence of models of co-operative education on PSO in Africa at South African tertiary institutions points towards a performance problem. According to Van Niekerk (1991:60) to solve, a performance problem such as the lack of ability to do a certain task is to give members additional knowledge, skills and attributes (KSAs).

For that reason, a much wider array of KSAs is required than is normally covered under general-purpose combat training. Broadening the KSA base through higher education is a means of shaping appropriate attitudes and setting the right expectations to help SA Army members and NGOs adapt to the demands of PSO. Langholtz, de Beer and Mostert (2003:7) acknowledge that direct supervision and field exercises are necessary to instruct hands-on technical skills. Yet, institutions of higher learning can provide co-operative education on PSO that are cognitive or knowledge based. This knowledge could include the UNITAR POCI courses, geo-political and security studies, international perceptions on PSO, international humanitarian law and the law of armed conflict, as well as other knowledge-based topics that peacekeepers need to understand in order to serve effectively on UN or AU missions.

The motivation for the research is evident from the discussion above and because no Institute of Higher Learning in South Africa is currently contributing to the field of PSO in Africa, this proposed Model of Co-operative Education on PSO in Africa could help to change the mindset of the major universities.

1.3.1 RESEARCH STATEMENT

A Model of Co-operative Education on PSO in Africa will satisfy the need for tertiary education, improved knowledge, changed attitudes and assist to solve conflict in Africa.

1.3.2 RESEARCH OBJECTIVES

The primary objectives for this research were to:

- Carry out a need analysis in order to determine whether there is a need among SA Army officers in the SANDF for a Model of Co-operative Education on PSO in Africa;
- Prepare an instructional design (ISD) report for a Model of Co-operative Education on PSO in Africa based on principles of scientific instructional design practice; and
- Draft curriculum content on PSO in accordance with the principles of curriculum design.

1.3.3 THE IMPORTANCE OF THE STUDY

The future continues to hold a high demographic risk of civil conflict in Africa. South Africa is in a state of transition and will remain as such for some time to come. The international community expects South Africa to become more involved in peacekeeping missions.

The SA Army, however, has a limited capacity to deploy troops in PSO over long periods. It has neither the logistical, nor the personnel capacity to do so. The defence budget remains under pressure to such an extent that South African military potency is slipping and will drop further if the lack of political will continues to hamper the effectiveness of the SA Army.

If South Africa wants to play a leading role on an unstable continent, it must have a focused and functional defence force. The expectation is that traditional training methods in the SA Army will not be able to satisfy all the present and future human resource development needs, especially the need for competent peacekeepers.

Within the overall educational philosophy of a combination of distance education and co-operative training, the nature of the proposed project is to fulfil the urgent need to change South African soldiers and other PSO stakeholders into unbiased diplomats.

Peacekeepers must be acquainted with the political, military and socio-cultural dynamics of the crisis area. UNITAR POCI, University of South Africa (UNISA) and the Central University of Technology, Free State (CUT), in collaboration with the SANDF, and institutions such as the ISS could use distance education andragogy to achieve the objectives of peace, security and economic stability in Southern Africa.

The focus of the SA Army from the onset should therefore be one of development in cooperation with other stakeholder organisations. Training peacekeepers via distance education is an inexpensive way for Institutions of Higher Learning to become involved and contribute. This could be a key step to assist in the development of a professional SANDF.

The researcher is of the opinion that a Model of Co-operative Education on PSO in Africa will provide training and education for a wide variety of learners, in order to improve their ability to participate in multinational peace support and humanitarian operations.

1.4   GENERAL RESEARCH DESIGN AND METHODOLOGY

1.4.1 <u>RESEARCH DESIGN</u>

The overall plan followed is a non-experimental design. Based on the four-dimensional framework, it becomes possible to categorise the study as one of an empirical nature using primary and secondary sources, numerical and textual data type with medium control (Mouton, 2001:146).

1.4.2 <u>POPULATION, SAMPLE AND SAMPLING</u>

The study included all officers in the SA Army (population) irrespective of rank, age or gender. In light of the size and complexity of the SANDF, the respondents (target population) selected from various units in the SA Army. A sample of approximately 90 officers randomly drawn from the SA Army reflects as closely as possible the characteristics of the entire population, although the selected sample can hardly ever be a mirror image of the population.

1.4.3 <u>DATA COLLECTION METHOD</u>

A survey determines the need for a higher learning programme and assists to analyse the target group. An instructional design model formed the blueprint for the design of the proposed learning programme and curriculum.

1.4.4 DATA ANALYSIS

The appropriate method for interpreting data will be descriptive statistics as described by SPSS computer software (SPSS, 1999). Data recorded as numerical values enables the analysis of data by statistical means. Measurement took place on an ordinal level in order to rank data in terms of a formulated order. Descriptive frequencies converted to percentages illustrate the levels of agreement.

1.5 OUTLINE OF THE RESEARCH REPORT

Besides this introductory chapter, the report is organised into a further four chapters.

Chapter 2, the literature review, contains the theoretical framework that has informed this research. The review involves the constructs of international peacekeeping, geo-politics and security studies, PSO in Africa, civil-military coordination and UNITAR POCI learning programs. Throughout the review, a theoretical basis for these constructs develop and it culminates in a summary from the material reviewed.

Chapter 3 discusses the methodology that formed the foundation of the research. The research strategy, sampling, measuring instruments, data collection procedure, data analysis and limitations of the study are discussed.

Chapter 4 presents the research results. Chapter 5 presents the conclusion and recommendations of this study. It argues the main findings by drawing together the results from the previous chapters into a programme strategy.

CHAPTER 2 - LITERATURE REVIEW

2.1   **INTRODUCTION**

This chapter contains the theoretical framework that has informed this research. The literature reviewed includes the doctrinal approaches of the United Kingdom (UK), United States of America (USA), and Nordic countries, Netherlands, France and Canada. The learning programs of UNITAR POCI, papers from the Institute of Strategic Studies (ISS), journals, newspapers and internet searches produced valuable information. The review demarcated to include learning programs, doctrine and papers on issues of geo-politics, security studies, civil-military coordination (CIMIC), and PSO.

The chapter starts with the definition of key concepts from a variety of viewpoints. The discussion begins with an overview of the approach to PSO during and post Cold War. It attempts to explain the evolution of peacekeeping operations during these periods and tries to illustrate the major consequences of doctrinal confusion.

Sections 1 is on international peacekeeping and discusses and compares the doctrine of the UK, Canada, USA, the Netherlands, France and the Nordic countries. For the potential peacekeeper in Africa it is important to have an international knowledge basis as starting point to project his/her own perspectives on PSO in Africa.

Section 2 gives an overview of geo-political and security matters in the international and national arena. This is necessary in order for the peacekeeper to understand the environment in which he/she is expected to operate.

Section 3 takes a brief look at PSO in Africa and the possible role of the SANDF in peace missions on the African continent. Section 4 discusses CIMIC and includes aspects of humanitarian operations. These are important issues, as the military is not the only role player in peace operations.

Section 5 introduces the UNITAR POCI system of correspondence instruction courses by giving an overview of the learning programmes available. The courses are of a generic nature and not aimed at a specific country or doctrine.

2.2   DEFINITION OF KEY CONCEPTS

Civilian and Military Cooperation (CIMIC) became necessary to find a mechanism that would improve interaction between civilians and the military (Hårleman, 2003:82), how civilian and military peacekeepers coordinate their efforts and work together to achieve the peace operations' mandate and goals (Standard Generic Training Module 10, 2003:1).

The resources and arrangements which support the relationship between commanders and the national authorities, civil and military, and civil populations in an area where military forces are or plan to be employed (Netherlands Ministry of Defence, 2000:332).

Conflict prevention is action taken to prevent disputes from developing between parties, to prevent existing disputes from escalating into conflicts and to limit the spread of the latter when they occur (Department of National Defence Canada, 2000:6-1).

Preventive actions can prevent a crisis developing into an armed conflict and can serve to stabilise and perhaps improve the economic and social situation in an affected area and prevent suffering (Netherlands Ministry of Defence, 2000:170).

Consent. UN Peace-keeping Operations are established with the consent and cooperation of the main parties involved in a conflict (Standard Generic Training Module 1B, 2003:13).

UN Peacekeeping operations are established with the consent and cooperation of the main parties involved in the conflict (Department of National Defence Canada, 2000:6-1).

Demobilisation is the opposite of recruiting combatants for an armed group. In the military sense, demobilisation entails either disbanding an armed unit, reducing the number of combatants in an armed group, or it represents an interim stage before reassembling entire armed forces (Gleichmann, Odenwald, Steenken and Wilkinson, 2004:15).

Reducing the level of armed forces personnel and equipment present in the area of operations to the levels agreed in a peace settlement (Netherlands Ministry of Defence, 2000:333).

Disaster relief operations in general aim at easing the living conditions for populations severely affected by a natural disaster (Hårleman: 2003: 81).

Disarmament refers primarily to the reduction and eventual elimination of weapons of mass destruction such as nuclear, chemical and biological weapons. Disarmament also refers to part of a demobilisation process often monitored by an international organisation (Hårleman, 2003:39).

Disarmament is the process whereby armed forces are relieved of their weapons in a controlled manner (Netherlands Ministry of Defence, 2000:333).

It is the assembly, control and disposal of weapons (Standard Generic Training Module 1B, 2003:13).

Humanitarian operations execute to relieve human suffering. Military humanitarian activities may accompany or be in support of humanitarian operations conducted by specialised civilian organisations (UK Ministry of Defence, 2004:1-1).

Most modern UN peacekeeping operations are deployed in response to complex emergencies. Complex emergencies usually imply large-scale human rights abuses, food shortages, and breakdown of basic social services like health and education, and people fleeing the conflict or searching for food and other basic needs, thus becoming refugees and/or internally displaced people (IDPs) (Standard Generic Training Module 9, 2003:3).

International Humanitarian Law (IHL) applicable to armed conflicts involves international rules established by treaty or custom, which are specifically intended to solve humanitarian problems that arise directly from international or non-international armed conflicts. For humanitarian reasons, these rules protect persons and property that are or may be affected by conflict (Bouvier, 2000:3).

Peace support operations (PSO) are multi-functional operations involving military forces and diplomatic humanitarian agencies. Their objective is to achieve humanitarian goals or a long-term political settlement and they are impartial in support of a UN mandate. This mandate includes peacekeeping, peace enforcement, conflict prevention, peacemaking, peace building and humanitarian operations (UK Ministry of Defence, 2004:1-1).

According to the Netherlands Ministry of Defence, (2000:333) PSO is impartial NATO military operations arising from an internationally recognised organisation's request for military assistance to retain, establish or enforce peace in an area or region.

The Norcaps PSO manual volume 1 (2002:41) describes PSO as multi-functional operations conducted impartially in support of a UN mandate involving military forces and diplomatic and humanitarian agencies and are designed to achieve to achieve a long-term political settlement or other conditions specified in the mandate.

The term PSO should be used to refer to all military activities in support of a peace mission. This includes military activities in support of predominantly political activities such preventative diplomacy, peacemaking and peace building (South African National Defence Force: 2005: 1-2).

Peace operations are military operations to support diplomatic efforts to reach a long-term political settlement and categorized as peacekeeping operations (PK) and peace enforcement operations (PE) (USA Department of Defence, 1995: 40).

Peacekeeping (PK) is a UN presence in the field, with the consent of the conflicting parties, to implement or monitor the implementations of arrangements relating to the control of conflicts and their resolution or to ensure the safe delivery of humanitarian relief (UN Department of Peacekeeping Operations, 1995:5).

Peacekeeping was developed as a series of ad hoc practical mechanism used by the UN to help contain armed conflicts and settle them by peaceful means. The mechanism devised by the UN to ensure international peace and security is outlined in Chapters VI, VII and VIII of the Charter (Standard Generic Training Module 1b, 2003:5).

PK is operations which, with the consent of the warring factions, support political activities to maintain or achieve peace (Netherlands Ministry of Defence, 2000:333).

PK operations are undertaken under chapter VI of the UN Charter and are conducted with the consent of all major parties to a conflict to monitor and control implementation of a peace agreement (UK Ministry of Defence, 2004:1-1).

Peacekeeping is the containment, moderation and /or termination of hostilities between or within states through various mediums to complement the political process of conflict resolution and to restore and maintain peace (Shaw and Cilliers, 1995:2).

PK are military operations undertaken with the consent of all major parties to a dispute, designed to monitor and facilitate implementation of an agreement (cease fire, truce, or other such agreements) and support diplomatic efforts to reach a long-term political settlement (USA Department of Defence, 1995: 40).

Peace enforcement operations (PE) restore peace between warring parties which, in principle, do not all consent to the intervention of a peace force (Netherlands Ministry of Defence, 2000:341).

The SANDF describes PE as activities where, in terms of Chapter VII of the UN Charter, it is necessary to use armed force to maintain or restore international peace and security in situations where peace is threatened. The use of armed force will only be authorised when all other peaceful means have failed (South African National Defence Force, 2005:1-3).

When all other efforts fail, Chapter VII of the Charter provides authority for enforcement, and includes the use of armed force to maintain or restore international peace and security (Department of National Defence Canada, 2000: 6-2).

According to Shaw and Cilliers, (1995:2) PE define under Chapter VII of the UN Charter as using military means to restore peace in an area of conflict.

PE operations are coercive operations undertaken under Chapter VII of the UN Charter and are conducted when the belligerent parties may not consent to intervention (UK Ministry of Defence, 2004:3).

PE is the application of military force, or threat of its use, normally pursuant to international authorization, to compel compliance with resolutions or sanctions designed to maintain or restore peace and order (USA Department of Defence, 1995: 41).

Peacemaking covers the diplomatic activities conducted after the commencement of a conflict aimed at establishing a cease-fire or a rapid peaceful settlement. They may include the provision of good offices, mediation, conciliation, diplomatic pressure, isolation and sanctions (UK Ministry of Defence, 2004:1-1).

Peacemaking is the range of diplomatic actions aimed at establishing a peaceful settlement once conflict is in progress or has resumed (Shaw and Cilliers, 1995:2).

Peacemaking is diplomatic action to bring hostile parties to negotiated agreements through peaceful means (Department of National Defence Canada, 2000: 6-1).

Peacemaking is a process of diplomacy, mediation, negotiation or other forms of peaceful consultation in order to end a conflict (Netherlands Ministry of Defence, 200:341).

Peacemaking is diplomatic actions to bring hostile parties to a negotiated agreement through peaceful means (The Norcaps PSO manual volume 1, 2002:41).

Peacemaking is the process of diplomacy, mediation, negotiation, or other forms of peaceful settlements that arranges an end to a dispute, and resolves issues that led to conflict (USA Department of Defence, 1995: 40).

Peace building is critical in the aftermath of conflict. It includes the identification and support of measures and structures that will promote peace and build trust and interaction among former enemies in order to avoid a relapse into conflict (UN Department of Peacekeeping Operations, 1995:5).

Peace building may occur at any stage in the conflict cycle, but is critical in the aftermath of a conflict. It includes activities such as the identification and support of measures and structures that will promote peace and build trust, and the facilitation of interaction among former enemies in order to prevent a relapse into conflict (South African National Defence Force, 2005:1-3).

Peace building is critical in the aftermath of conflict. It includes the identification and support of measures and structures, which will promote peace and build trust and interaction among former enemies, in order to avoid a relapse into conflict (Department of National Defence Canada, 2000: 6-2).

Peace building is actions taken after conflict to identify and support structures that strengthen and solidify a peace settlement in order to avoid a relapse into conflict (Shaw and Cilliers, 1995:3).

Preventive diplomacy involves diplomatic steps which are in effect taken before an expected crisis and are designed to remove the cause of the conflict. The aim is to prevent the use of force. Preventive measures may also be taken to prevent the spread or intensification of the limited use of force. Conflict prevention operations such as the preventive deployment of units can support the process with military assets (Netherlands Ministry of Defence, 2000:16).

Preventive diplomacy is action to prevent disputes arising between parties, to prevent existing disputes from escalating into conflicts, and to limit the spread of the latter when they occur (UK Ministry of Defence, 2004:1-1).

Preventive diplomacy consists of diplomatic actions taken in advance of a predictable crisis to prevent or limit violence (USA Department of Defence, 1995: 41).

<u>Reintegration</u> is defined here as the process by which ex-combatants acquire civilian status and gain access to civilian forms of work and income. It is essentially a social and economic process with an open time frame, primarily taking place in communities at local level. It forms part of the general development of a country and a national responsibility often necessitating external assistance (Gleichmann et al. 2004:15).

2.3   **DISCUSSION**

Consent is one of the important keystones of peacekeeping. Since the end of the Cold War, (1989-1990), however, peacekeeping has changed fundamentally. Peacekeeping no longer limit only to military operations conducted with the consent of all major parties to a conflict to monitor and control implementation of a peace agreement. These changes have had major implications as concepts such as consent, no longer have a universally accepted meaning.

From the definition of key concepts it is clear that terms and definitions concerning PSO are sometimes mixed up whether talking political or military language. This leads to misunderstandings (Norcaps PSO manual volume 1, 2002:40).

Distinctions between concepts are often unclear (Shaw and Cilliers, 1995:2). Within the PSO arena, experience has shown that different Government Departments and agencies, including vitally important Non-Governmental Organisations (NGO's) frequently use the same terms and phrases but ascribe different meanings to them (South African National Defence Force, 2005:1-2).

In the absence of a uniform peacekeeping doctrine within the UN, different nations tend to emphasise different aspects of concepts. It is impossible to have a coherent peacekeeping mission, when troop contributors fail to agree on the purpose, strategy, and conduct of an operation. The challenge to multi-national PSO is thus obvious (Potgieter, 1996:1).

The development of UN peacekeeping divide in two distinct periods: during the Cold War (1945 to 1988) and post Cold War after 1989. The founders of the UN had not foreseen the possibility of engaging in peacekeeping operations; thus, it is not mentioned at all in the original UN Charter. However, just after World War II, tensions between the USA and the Soviet Union, known as the Cold War, emerged and significantly affected the operation of the UN. As a result of the increasing disagreement between the two superpowers, the original collective security system, which was based on peace enforcement by the Security Council and consensus by major powers, became unworkable. This led to the conception of peacekeeping (Liu, 1999: 1-123).

'First generation' operations, typical of the first forty years of UN peacekeeping, were characterised by unarmed or lightly armed troops. Peacekeepers deployed to stabilise cease-fires between the regular armies of states, while trying to find a political solution. These operations were predicated on the consent of the warring parties, and dependent for success on the neutrality and impartiality of a UN force, which would only use arms to defend their lives or their mandate (Malan, 1996:3).

Before 1989, a gradual evolution of peacekeeping concepts is observable, as well as continuity in participating countries that trained their troops in the tasks of peacekeeping. The product of this development, the training and the continuity brought about by regular participants, is an unambiguous joint UN peacekeeping approach. The major troop contributing countries formed a significant consensus about what peacekeeping is and when to use it during the period preceding 1989 (Cilliers, 1996:2).

A fundamental change came about in 1989. 'Second generation' operations, after the Cold War presented the opportunity to end proxy Cold War conflicts through negotiated settlements. The UN and/or other multinational organisations guided the adversaries to political settlements based on compromise (Namibia, Cambodia, El Salvador, Mozambique and Angola). The UN became involved in ending internal conflicts through a multi-dimensional process that included activities such as the separation of combatants; the disarmament of irregular forces; the demobilisation and transformation of regular and irregular forces into a unified army; the establishment of new policing systems; and the monitoring of elections for new governments (Malan 1996:3).

So after forty years of relative clarity on the role and functions of UN peacekeeping, the 1990s have witnessed a peacekeeping debate of such complexity that it is difficult to figure out exactly what 'peacekeeping' is all about (Malan 1998:3).

Almost all of the post Cold War missions have been spoiled by ambiguous mandates, that may imply forceful action to enforce a settlement, without an clear command or the provision of appropriate troops and resources to use such a forceful approach (Cilliers, 1996:4).

The challenges and risks of peacekeeping missions after 1989 differ dramatically from prior ones. 'Third generation' missions presently take place during civil wars that are far more difficult to resolve than interstate wars, and have a multitude of first-time political, humanitarian, and military components. These factors produced an unusual degree of complexity, volatility, and vulnerability for PSO in the 1990s.

Not only has the nature of peacekeeping tasks changed, the participants in peacekeeping operations have also changed. Until 1988, UN peacekeeping had a regular pool of contributing nations, consisting of the core states of Canada, Ireland, Italy, Australia and the Nordic countries (Finland, Norway, Sweden and Denmark). Canada is the only member state that has participated in all thirteen peacekeeping operations between 1948 and 1987. In the missions undertaken between 1989 and October 1993, the role-players changed. Canada remains the only country to participate in every UN peacekeeping mission and the rate of participation by the Nordic countries, Ireland, Australia and Italy remains high. However, during this period Argentina participated in nine operations, France in eight operations, being the largest troop contributor during this time, the US and Austria each in seven operations, Russia in six operations, and the UK in four operations (Huldt, 1995: 106-107).

Currently, UN peacekeeping personnel come from 112 countries with the top 10 troop contributors: Pakistan, Bangladesh, India, Jordan, Nepal, Ghana, Uruguay, Ethiopia, Nigeria and South Africa. Over 67 percent of all UN military and police personnel come form the developing nations and less than 5.8 percent from the EU and about 0.5 percent from the USA (Deen, 2006:5).

These new contributing states have brought with them the complications arising from inadequate experience in peacekeeping missions. They often utilise idiosyncratic definitions of key terms, and adopt competing ideas of what peacekeeping is and how to execute it.

The infusion of new states in PSO and the changed tasks of peacekeeping have led to a proliferation of national peacekeeping doctrines. In order to understand how these doctrines deviate from traditional notions of UN peacekeeping, section one discusses and compares the peacekeeping approach of the Nordic countries, UK, Netherlands, Canada, USA and France.

2.3.1 **SECTION 1: PSO FROM AN INTERNATIONAL PERSPECTIVE**

2.3.1.1 Nordic PSO

The Nordic countries were regular participants in PSO before 1989. During the Cold War period the concept of peacekeeping was well defined and all participating parties had consensus. This suggests that their doctrine embrace traditional peacekeeping as described in the Nordic tactical manual of 2002 and is developed for use by Nordic troops.

The manual volume 1 and 2 by Buur, Vienola, Ohlsson and Terp (2002:5), is based on previous Nordic experience of UN and other PSO up to 2001. The aim of the manual is to standardise PSO tactics and techniques.

The Nordic approach to PSO includes the consent of the parties, neutrality and impartiality and the use of weapons in self-defence only. Peacekeepers are neutral observers and do not take part in hostilities (ibid, p.25).

Neutrality implies not taking sides in a conflict situation. The consent of parties is crucial to the success of peacekeepers in accomplishing their mission, because it signals the willingness of parties to cooperate. To maintain the consent of belligerent parties, peacekeepers must remain neutral and impartial. If one of the parties perceives that peacekeepers are taking sides, consent may be withdrawn and hostilities may start again, and peacekeepers might come under attack. Concepts such as the non-use of arms, negotiation and mediation are basic principles to restore a situation of peace.

The Nordic approach to the use of force is that if force is to be used, the extent and range will be confined to what is strictly necessary. This approach is based on the experience of many UN operations and the principle that force generates force. By using more force than strictly necessary, the danger will be that tensions rises and the possibility of negotiations will lessen (ibid, p.55).

The Nordic countries have rejected the view that there is a grey area between peacekeeping and peace enforcement. According to them, the two kinds of operations clearly divide by the absence or presence of consent by the warring parties, and the limited use of force in self-defence (ibid, p.69).

2.3.1.2   United Kingdom (UK)

UK doctrine focuses more at the operational level. It concentrates on broad concepts and principles and is not intended to be prescriptive, recognising that doctrine has not been fully tested and is likely to require revision (UK, Ministry of Defence, 2004: V).

The UK took the basic peacekeeping philosophy in the Nordic Manuals and attempted to stretch it for adaptation by full-time professional armies, and to make it more robust and suitable for the more uncertain circumstances in which forces found themselves more frequently operating.

The UK military first defined PSO to cover PK and PE operations, but is now use it more widely to embrace not only PK and PE, but also those other peace related operations, for example, conflict prevention, peace making, peace building and humanitarian operations. UK PSO is increasingly in response to complex intra-state conflicts involving widespread human rights violations as opposed to more traditional PK. Such complex emergencies require a composite response, involving diplomatic and humanitarian agencies. According to UK doctrine without the active and willing involvement of the Host Nation, there can be no self-sustaining peace. UK military activities are conducted with either a PK or PE profile (ibid, p.1-1).

UK PSO considerations unavoidably draw to the fundamentals of consent, impartiality and their relationship with the application of force. Firstly, peacekeeping is dependent on the consent of the parties and the promotion of co-operation. The general notion that there is a boundary of consent, however, is only perceived as being relevant from the perspective of a lightly armed PK force.

45

For a combat-capable PSO force, consent is an important consideration but not as a boundary which cannot be easily and frequently recrossed. From a broader PSO force perceptive, there is no border line of consent. The concept of neutrality shifted to one of impartiality. The key difference is that neutrality suggests observation and passivity, while impartiality requires principled judgements in relation to the mandate and endorses consequential impartial responses (Wilkinson, 1998:6).

The British approach to the use of force evolved from 'no use of force' to 'minimum use of force', to 'minimum necessary use of force'. The British see the need to define the grey area between peacekeeping and war, so as to offer policymakers a wider range of more appropriate options (ibid, p.8).

2.3.1.3   Netherlands

This publication focuses primarily on the actions at the operational and tactical level by formations (brigade, division) and units (battalions). It also gives guidance for operations at the lower levels, thus presenting a cohesive picture of peace operations (Amersfoort, Roozenbeek and Klep, 1999:13).

The Netherlands use allied joint doctrine, the military concept for the North Atlantic Treaty Organisation (NATO) on PSO and the British joint warfare publication on PSO as a common foundation for operating in a NATO context. The Royal Netherlands Army operate in peace operations in a multinational setting, adhering to two relevant international approaches, namely that of the UN and that of NATO. These approaches can be regarded as complementary. The ability to work together (interoperability) during peace operations are thus enhanced (ibid, p.14).

Doctrine promotes a military approach to peace operations. The Netherlands doctrine differentiates between peacekeeping operations and acknowledges that it has changed considerably over the years. A distinction has therefore been made between traditional ('first-generation') and new ('second-generation') peacekeeping operations.

First-generation peacekeeping operations are operations in which an international organisation deploys a force between two or more (warring) parties who consent to this action. This gives the international community the opportunity to seek a political solution to the conflict. The activities of the peace force are mainly concentrated on the prevention of hostilities and, if possible, establishing a dialogue between the parties (ibid, p.74)

Second-generation peacekeeping operations are usually operations in which troops are deployed, again with the consent of the parties involved, in support of a political solution and to supervise the observance of a peace settlement. In second-generation operations, the force operates throughout the conflict area and not just in a buffer zone (ibid, p.75).

As far as the desired end state is concerned, the distinction between peacekeeping and peace-enforcing is irrelevant. Both are, after all, intended to achieve the same goal: a stable situation with a good chance of peace for the long term. The distinguishing criterion is the consent to the presence of and operations by the peace force.

This criterion would appear in itself to be clear, employable and measurable, but the situations in practice are usually less clear and difficult to assess. Thus there may indeed be consent at the strategic level (the national government or the leaders of a party) or at the operational level (local authorities and commanders of large units or formations), but at the tactical level (the local 'warlord', the mayor or the police), consent and cooperation may not be forthcoming as a result of a disturbed balance of power in one of the parties. There may also be a difference between the degree of consent which has been achieved at the political level and the extent of compliance with the peace agreement at the executive level. This means that the distinction between peacekeeping and peace-enforcing can be extremely blurred (ibid, p.78).

The doctrine is based mainly on the promotion of confidence and cooperation. Both aspects thus have a direct impact on the degree of consent to the presence of and actions by the peace force. A primary condition for consent is the possibility of clearly identifying the parties in the conflict, which need to give their consent. The degree of consent can be subject to frequent and sudden change. If consent to the operation is doubtful, direct efforts must be made at all levels to stabilise and promote this consent. Ideally, this is done through dialogue and by peaceful means. Political pressure, sanctions, the threat of force or the controlled use of force are options. Once the boundary between peacekeeping and peace-enforcing has been crossed, the capacity for a credible degree of force is essential for the success of the operation. One must bear in mind, however, that this is a peace support operation and not a war. This means that any loss of consent must be won back. This is extremely difficult to put into practice, which means that it will not be easy for the peace force to rebuild a bond of trust and good cooperation with the parties. For a peacekeeping power which has lost consent across the board, the chance of implementing the mandate is virtually nonexistent; the only remaining option for the force is to withdraw from the theatre of operations (ibid, p.82).

Two basic principles are important for restraint or minimum necessary force: necessity and proportionality. Necessity means that force may only be used if it is essential in order to achieve the military objective and other means are inadequate. Proportionality means that force must be kept to the minimum level needed to achieve that objective. Both principles set limitations on where, when and to what extent troops may use force. Unnecessary use of force has an adverse effect on the impartiality and credibility of the troops. Excessive force may jeopardise the consent of the parties in the conflict and the chances of long-term success.

These principles must not, incidentally, be taken to mean that troops should refrain from using force altogether. If the situation so demands, they should certainly not hesitate to use force. In any event, the right of self-defence applies at all times. Any use of force beyond this, for example to secure freedom of movement, must be authorised by the rules of engagement (ibid, p.96).

2.3.1.4   <u>USA - Military Operations other than War (MOOTW)</u>

This publication provides basic concepts and principles to guide the services and combatant commands to prepare for and conduct MOOTW. MOOTW focus on deterring war, resolving conflict, promoting peace, and supporting civil authorities in response to domestic crises (USA Joint Doctrine, J3 - MOOTW: 1995: 13).

According to USA doctrine MOOTW principles are an extension of war fighting doctrine. Although MOOTW and war may often seem similar in action, MOOTW focus on deterring war and promoting peace while war encompasses large-scale, sustained combat operations. MOOTW are more sensitive to political considerations and often the military may not be the primary role player. More restrictive rules of engagement are followed (ibid, p.10).

MOOTW include arms control, combating terrorism, Department of Defence support to counter-drug operations, enforcement of sanctions/maritime intercept operations, enforcing exclusion zones, ensuring freedom of navigation and over-flight, humanitarian assistance, military support to civil authorities, nation assistance/support to counterinsurgency, non-combatant evacuation operations, protection of shipping, recovery operations, show of force operations, strikes and raids, support to insurgency and peace operations (PO) (ibid, p:25).

PO is military operations to support diplomatic efforts to reach a long-term political settlement and categorized as PK and PE. American doctrine also differentiates between these types op PO. PK Operations are military operations undertaken with the consent of all major parties to a dispute, designed to monitor and facilitate implementation of an agreement and support diplomatic efforts to reach a long-term political settlement (ibid, p.40). The American view of PK upholds the importance of neutrality, impartiality, and minimal use of force.

Joint forces support PE operations to compel compliance with measures designed to establish an environment for cease fire. PE is the application of military force, or threat of its use, normally pursuant to international authorization, to compel compliance with resolutions or sanctions designed to maintain or restore peace and order. PE missions include intervention operations, as well as operations to restore order, enforce sanctions, forcibly separate belligerents, and establish and supervise exclusion zones for the purpose of establishing an environment for cease-fire. Unlike PK, such operations do not require the consent of the states involved or of other parties to the conflict (ibid, p.41).

USA doctrine observe a grey area between PK and PE in which cease fires break down, factions withdraw their consent, and new political entities emerge that had no part in the original granting of consent to the PK operation. The existence of a possible grey area means that a force operating in the grey area should be configured to be able to operate as a peace enforcer even when the mandate is more limited (Cilliers, 1996:10).

2.3.1.5   Canada

Canadian doctrine embraces the seven categories (preventive deployment, peacemaking, peacekeeping, peace-enforcement, peace building, sanctions and disarmament) the UN has set forth for future efforts to restore peace and security. According to Canadian doctrine these seven concepts reflect the growing scope and complexity of UN activities and provide a useful insight into how the world can more fully embrace and achieve the objectives of the UN Charter (Department of National Defence Canada. 2000: 6-1).

Canadian doctrine distinguishes between PK and PE. PK is a UN presence in the field, with the consent of the parties, to implement or monitor the implementation of arrangements relating to the control of conflicts and their resolution or to ensure the safe delivery of humanitarian relief. PE on the other hand may be needed when all other efforts fail. The authority for enforcement is provided by Chapter VII of the Charter and includes the use of armed force to maintain or restore international peace and security in situations where there is a threat to peace, breach of peace or an act of aggression (ibid, p.6-2).

The doctrine promulgate that UN peacekeeping operations are established with the consent and the cooperation of the main parties involved in the conflict. A UN Force must be impartial in character. The Canadians believe that the force cannot take sides without becoming part of the conflict (ibid, p.6-2).

The use of force is based on the reasonable belief that a threat exists warranting the use of force. Force must never be more than the minimum necessary to carry out and accomplish assigned objectives or the mission. Deadly force is justified only under conditions of extreme necessity and as a last resort when all lesser means have failed or cannot reasonably be employed (ibid, p.14-1).

Chapters of importance in this doctrine that do not feature in sufficient detail in other PSO publications include hostage survival, the operations centre, peace partners, preventative medicine and stress management (ibid, p.12-1, 17-1, 24-1, 25-1, 26-1).

2.3.1.6   French Peacekeeping

Where other doctrine shows a clear lineage to the traditional, the French demonstrate few misgivings in trying to invent something new. French doctrine refers to France's colonial heritage and suggests that its experience in policing its colonies is applicable to the challenges of PK today (French Ministry of Defence, nd, op cit).

The French divide peace missions into three: PK, peace-restoring, and PE. PE is intervention with consent of the parties to maintain peace where hostilities have stopped, carried out under Chapter VI of the UN Charter. Both peace-restoring and PE occur where war is still being waged, but differ in one respect. In PE a party is designated to be the aggressor in the conflict and must be defeated with force (Cilliers, 1996:9).

Unlike Nordic or British doctrines that require soldiers to have specific PK training, the French doctrine anticipate that fighting instruction and training is the major part of preparing troops for a peace mission (ibid, p.9).

The French label for the principle that should guide their PK operations is "active impartiality". For the French, impartiality is to be determined in relation to the warring parties' compliance with the mandate of an operation. The French consider the mandate a law, and believe that it is the military's role to act as judge and police in ensuring that all parties live up to the law (ibid, p.9).

The French draw a clear distinction between impartiality and neutrality. While a PK force must be impartial, it must not be neutral to some of the actions of the parties present. Impartiality, as a commitment to make parties live up to the mandate, means that some of the behaviour and actions of the parties present must stop or change. Moreover, the monitoring, judging, and policing of the mandate must be active if it wants to be credible (ibid, p.9).

2.3.1.7   Comparison of Doctrines and Approaches

The researcher used the following dimensions in the comparison of approaches and doctrine: the definition of PSO, responses to non-compliance, and the use of force.

Definition of PSO

British and Netherlands doctrine defines various types of PO under the umbrella term of PSO (conflict prevention, peace making, peace building and humanitarian operations). USA doctrine uses the term MOOTW which besides peace missions include 15 other operations than war. Nordic and Canadian doctrine do not use the umbrella term PSO, either, but address peacekeeping and peace-enforcement separately.   French doctrine divides peace missions into three, namely: peacekeeping, peace-restoring, and peace enforcement.

However, Nordic, British, American, Dutch, and Canadian doctrine agree what constitutes PK: the dividing line between PK and some of the other peace operations is the consent of the parties, the importance of neutrality and impartiality, and the limited use of force in self-defence. French doctrine differs in that it defines impartiality in terms of the mandate and promulgate that force can be used to force compliance. It acknowledges that the use of force may endanger the perceived neutrality of the force, but defines it as an acceptable risk.

For the Dutch, as far as the desired end state is concerned, the distinction between PK and PE is irrelevant as both intend to achieve the same goal, making a distinction between PK and PE smudged. The Canadian, British, Nordic and American approaches include the use of armed force to maintain or restore international peace and security. The Americans distinguish PE from war. PE is the application of military force, or threat of its use, in order to induce compliance with resolutions designed to restore peace and order. The French concept of peace restoration is thus closer to the American notion of PE, since there is no politically identified enemy. The French notion of PE, on the other hand, is essentially war.

Response to Non-compliance

Both the American and British doctrines, as well as the Nordic approach, agree on how PK should deal with non-compliance by parties who have signed agreements. If the mission has been defined as PK, the only appropriate response to non-compliance by the parties is to observe report and mediate among them. No attempt should be made to compel compliance, either through the use or threat of force, for that would cross the line that separates PK from PE. Impartiality and neutrality do not imply tentativeness in calling attention to violations or cheating by parties, but it does mean that compliance cannot be compelled. The French doctrine defines impartiality in terms of the mandate, not the parties. PK not only involves observing and reporting violations and mediating between the parties when violations occur, but using or threatening force to compel the parties to fulfil their obligations to the mandate when negotiating fails. The French acknowledge that, in holding the parties to their obligations, their neutrality may be jeopardised.

Use of Force

British and Nordic view is categorical: the use of force, if for anything other than self-defence, is likely to escalate violence and discourage compliance with the mandate, because the mission loses its neutrality and legitimacy. The American view leans to that position: it warns of the escalating potential of the use of force. The French doctrine departs from an opposite position and warns of the potential adverse effects of the decision not to use violence. The French position is that the failure of parties to implement their agreements is as likely to result from the unwillingness of the peacekeepers to use force to induce commitment.

Doctrinal Issues

According to Cilliers (1996:13), the examples of Somalia and Bosnia confirm the potential damaging effects of competing doctrines in PK missions. When key contributing states differ on such issues as the importance of consent, the efficiency of the use of force and the need for impartiality and neutrality, the result is likely to be an incoherent and ineffective peace operation.

Also it is clear that the application of traditional PK to situations that do not meet the pre-requisites for PK has had dire consequences in countries such as Bosnia, Somalia and Rwanda. These examples cast doubt on whether traditional PK are relevant in today's unpredictable peacekeeping situations, the so called 'third generation' operations.

In the volatile peacekeeping environment of the 1990s, doctrinal unity among troop contributing countries was important for mission success. Where the UN was successful, it was due in part to the ability of forces to agree on the appropriate rules of conduct of their mission.

Doctrine for peace operations should begin by acknowledging that these operations take place in environments where consent can disappear overnight, may decay over the course of a mission, or may be present at the theatre level, but not at the operational level. Therefore, doctrine should deal with the question of how best to plan, equip and behave under such circumstances.

The key issue is whether it is sensible or damaging to enter into the implementation of civil war agreements, in the light of the ambiguities and short-lived nature of consent.

As having restricted PK doctrine to operations where there is peace to keep and having identified that PE is different from war, it has been possible to define PE and offer guidance for its conduct. The doctrinal approach for PE should offer maximum flexibility in the conduct of operations, offering a wide range of enforcement and consent-promoting techniques (Wilkinson, 1998:7).

The conduct of operations will rely heavily on information operations and other techniques designed to persuade the warring parties that their best interests lie in peace rather than a return to conflict. When and if one of the warring parties fails to comply with the mandate and it becomes necessary for the PSO contingent to use force, the aim would be to re-enforce the peace rather than the physical defeat of the non-complying party (ibid, p.7).

Military efforts that build consent must coordinate into a wider multi-agency 'hearts and minds' strategy. Military actions should end conflict by conciliation rather than a short term and superficial conclusion of the conflict by force. Assisting the host nation to establish a stable and self-sustaining peace, not military victory, is the ultimate measure of success in PSO (ibid, p.8).

Military forces may need to conduct combat operations to enforce compliance, but the use of force will be restricted by the long-term requirement to rebuild consent and by the needs of peace building in general. In the conduct of PSO, military forces must be prepared to be placed in support of a civilian agency. It is the responsibility of this head of mission, not of the military force commander, to develop and co-ordinate the mission plan, although the latter will make a significant input into its development (ibid. p.8).

The fundamental question, what is so different about modern operations in complex emergencies – so-called "grey zones"? The answer is in a close examination of the desired end-state of these various operations. Inevitably, the end-state focused on security issues, the creation of conditions in which civilian agencies could redress the causes of the complex emergency and the creation of a self-sustaining peace, rather than the defeat of an opposing force.

Military actions need to be designed to create a secure environment and conditions in which others can build a self-sustaining peace, rather than a on the surface ending of conflict by military force. This suggests doctrine to identify and define an approach to PSO balanced against the long term requirements of peace-building. It is clear that a doctrine separate from war fighting, while acknowledging that the ability to escalate and use force remains a prerequisite in PSO.

Next, there is a broad discussion on geo-politics and security, as it is important that the peacekeeper should have knowledge of the battle space environment in which he/she is going to operate.

2.3.2 **SECTION 2: GEO-POLITICS AND SECURITY**

The Elements of a Geo-political Study

A state exists to protect, foster and give political expression to the nation. Geo-politics, therefore, is the study of the differences, which exist between states. The decision makers in any given state must possess power. If they do not, they would not be able to occupy and retain their decision-making role. Political power in the international sphere classifies as military, economic and power over opinion. Military power is the ultimate basis of power. Power to wage war is dependent upon the geographical factors - location and area, population, resources and industry. The physical attributes of a state include the following: location, size, shape, boundaries and the territorial sea, climate, surface configuration, soils and natural vegetation, as well as water features (SANDF SANWC: nd: 1-82). These elements, taken separately and in combination with one another, are of significance in the study of geo-politics, in Africa.

The economic climate in a poor, underdeveloped Africa is a natural breeding ground for evolutionary influences that create instability. No portion of the world today accommodates poorer, more dependent nations than Africa (Papp, 1988:129-130).

The communication systems of the continent leave much to desire and the shortage of good and adequate roads, railways and air communications restricts the economic development and progress of all states (ibid, p 130).

The considerable stress caused by relatively little arable land hastens the process of urbanisation. The "cities", however, are not in a position economically fit to absorb all these people, with the result that slums develop, which leads to unstable conditions (ibid, p.130).

The high population growth rate in Africa in general has led to pessimism over Africa's inability to win the fight against illiteracy. Illiteracy in Africa estimates to be as high as 74%. Human development can only occur with good health. Yet, most people in the poverty-stricken regions of the third world suffer from a combination of longstanding malnutrition, HIV/AIDS, Tuberculosis (TB) and other diseases, which, in turn, affect productivity (ibid, p. 130).

The political climate in Africa has made the economic dilemma on the continent worse rather than better. Pan-African aspirations and promises of freedom have only brought frustration (Africa Contemporary Record, 1981:97).

However, Africa as a whole assumed new and greater relevance for political action by external actors, inline with African interests and the long-term interests of the international community. The interest in Africa is in many respects, not with peace and security per se, but with threats faced by third parties (USA, Europe and China) as well as their concrete interests such as energy supply and migration (Klingebiel, 2005: 39).

It is necessary to bear in mind that Africa is the home of various important raw materials, which are of vital importance in an industrial world. Africa is becoming an increasingly important factor in global energy markets. It currently contributes 12 percent of the world's oil production. With instability in other oil-producing regions and the rising energy demands of China and India, Africa is an increasingly attractive resource (Wolfe, 2005: 1-4).

The aforementioned paragraphs gave a brief insight into social, political, and economic climate of the African continent. Although generalised it gives the peacekeeper a broad overview of the African battle space conditions. The next few paragraphs provide a short discussion of the security – development nexus concerning international politics, Africa and RSA studies.

International Politics

The major political actors in the world have been trying to find ways to a new formula of stability following the collapse of the bipolar framework set up by the Cold War. After the fall of the Soviet Union in 1989-1990, the conventional wisdom had it that the USA was the sole remaining "superpower," bringing the possibility of a unipolar order (Weinstein, 2004:1).

Through the 1990s, a new paradigm of world order seemed to be emerging put concisely by the term "globalisation." Globalisation signalled a comprehensive transformation of social organisation in which peaceful economic competition would replace military conflict (ibid, p.1).

However, a complex political world also harbours opposing tendencies such as Islamic revolutionaries, reactionary nationalism, HIV/AIDS crisis, failed states, resource wars in Africa, an unresolved conflict between Israel and Palestine. The attacks on the World Trade Centre and Pentagon on September 11, 2001, brought forward Islamic revolution as a threat to world security (ibid, p.2).

The initial response to the attacks was an invasion of Afghanistan to remove al-Qaeda and depose the Taliban regime. The decision by the Bush administration to effect regime change in Iraq militarily accompany in the present period of a drift toward multipolarity. Nuclear proliferation in states outside and within the globalisation system is a major concern (ibid, p.2).

The major threat in the new environment of uncertainty is the spread of militarization around the world, as regional powers grid themselves to advance and defend their interests. Remember that the USA is powerful but it is not invincible...it needs the help of other countries (Van der Westhuizen, 2005: 3).

Africa Studies

The events of September 11, 2001, had severe consequences for African development and security. With world attention focused on the so-called "war on terror", Africa's development and security concerns have taken a backseat despite assurances that the continent's problems will not be edited from the international agenda (Daniels, 2005:3).

In all other regions of the world, the incidence of civil war has been on a broadly declining trend over the past thirty years, but in Africa, the long-term trend has been upwards (Collier, 2004:1).

Africa's wars in the 1990s were all very different in their specifics. Nevertheless, they share a number of important characteristics. Firstly, one of the main underlying causes of these wars was the weakness, corruption, high level of militarization and, in some cases, the complete collapse, of the states involved. Secondly, they all involved multiple belligerents fighting for a variety of often shifting economic and political motivations. Thirdly, they all had serious regional dimensions and regional implications. Fourthly they were all remarkable for the brutality of the tactics (ranging from mass murder and ethnic cleansing, amputation, starvation, forced labour, rape and cannibalism) used by belligerents to secure their strategic objectives (Porteous, 2004: 1-5).

For the near future, the highest demographic risks of civil conflict remain concentrated in sub-Saharan Africa (Cincotta et al. 2003:13).

However, for perhaps the first time in a generation, Africa presents a picture of hope – although it differs from region to region. The AU and Africa as a whole have accepted the concept of NEPAD. NEPAD is a state-centric initiative, pitched at the level of African political leadership taking responsibility for the continents development. The five core principles of NEPAD are good governance; entrenchment of democracy, peace, stability and security; sound economic policy-making and execution; productive partnerships; and domestic ownership and leadership (Cilliers, 2004:5-50).

RSA Studies

South Africa forms an integral part of Africa and its footprints on the political, economic, social and humanitarian landscape are experienced and appreciated around the continent (Daniels, 2005:1-9).

The end of apartheid in South Africa has considerably increased prospects for security in southern Africa. South Africa's memberships in SADC and the AU, as well as efforts to mediate in conflicts across Africa have highlighted its new role as a stabilising and mediating force (Klasen and Zulu, nd: 43-62).

The changing security environment requires a multi-disciplinary approach to conflict resolution, incorporating the "political, economic, social, cultural and personal security... (In addition) that appropriate responses...must include a focus on effective governance, robust democracies and continuous economic and social development (Cilliers, 1999:1-16).

With no short-term solutions or 'quick fixes' for many of the conflicts on the continent, South Africa will have to carefully choose which resources to deploy, where these resources are most required and which environment best reflects its national interests. The SANDF will always be expected and compelled to act in accordance with the Constitution and the principles of international law regulating the use of force, notwithstanding the nature or the place of operations (SA Ministry of Defence Instruction, 2001:1-15). Military strategy consists of the establishment of military objectives, the formulation of military strategic concepts to accomplish the objectives and the use of military resources to implement the concepts. When any of these basic elements is incompatible with the others, national security may be in danger (Lykke, 1997: 183-186).

To conclude, accept that development is inevitably a slow process. There is no recipe for overnight success. In due course clearer distinctions will emerge between capitalism and socialism in Africa and in the relative performance of both in meeting the challenge of development. It is important for the professional military officer to understand the dynamics of the geo-politics in order to analyse the battle space. It is also important for him/her to understand the political, social and economic dynamics of Africa and the factors that could threaten the security and stability of the region. Next, the researcher briefly discusses PSO in the African context.

2.3.2   **SECTION 3: PSO IN AFRICA**

Geopolitical developments over the past ten years have triggered a new type of conflict. The end of the Cold War brought several proxy wars to a close, but it also meant that weak states have become more vulnerable to internal strife and, in some cases, disintegrated into failed states torn apart by armed combat between hosts of local power centres (Studer, 2001: 367-391).

One of the most disturbing features of these new conflicts is that, very often, civilians are no longer "caught in the crossfire," but deliberately targeted on account of their group identity. The high price paid by the civilian population and the destabilisation of entire regions have given rise to a greater need for military intervention to restore peace and security (ibid, p367-391).

Some of the most challenging conflicts in the world at the moment are in Africa: the crisis in the Darfur region of Sudan and less-than-transparent governments and ongoing uncertainty in Sierra Leone, Angola and the Democratic Republic of the Congo (DRC), for example. In many cases, the developed world watches these conflicts develop, as in the 1994 Rwandan genocide, and does nothing to intervene. When it did intervene, most often in the form of a UN peacekeeping mission, the results have been mixed. Some projects have succeeded, while many have failed to suppress violence or restore order in the countries to which they deployed. By the start of 2005, the UN had led seven peace operations in Africa: in Burundi, the Ivory Coast, the Democratic Republic of the Congo (DRC), Ethiopia/Eritrea, Liberia, Sierra Leone and the western Sahara, with an eighth operation planned for Sudan (ibid, p.367-391).

Regional groups such the Economic Community of West African States (ECOWAS) and the AU are focusing on building their own capacity to carry out peacekeeping operations in Africa. The UN and western nations support the conduct of theses missions, and are happy to have African soldiers patrolling African conflicts (ibid, p.367-391).

Many factors contributed to the need for peacekeeping missions in Africa, not least the continent's history of colonialism and conflict. The end of the Cold War coincided with the collapse of state institutions in countries such as Liberia, Somalia, Sierra Leone and the Congo (DRC). Disputes over natural resources, diamonds in Sierra Leone and gold and cobalt in the DRC, led to armed conflict that evolved into guerilla warfare involving mercenaries, warlords, militias and child soldiers (Pan, 2005: 1-15).

A massive influx of weapons and small arms from Eastern Europe since the 1990s feed the conflicts in Africa. The unrest and armed violence in many African countries with no central governing authority cause instability that often spilled over borders. This is particularly true in West Africa, where longstanding cultural and trade ties cross national lines (ibid, p.1-15).

The AU models on the European Union (EU) and aims at promoting democracy, human rights and economic development across Africa. The AU relies on regional bodies such as ECOWAS and SADC to provide forces and support for

PK operations. The AU's Peace and Security Council is overseeing the establishment of a permanent African security force, known as the Africa Standby Force (ASF) (ibid, 1-15).

By 2010, the AU plans to have five or six brigades of 5,000 troops each, stationed around Africa, and able to respond to any unrest. The international community, including the Group of Eight (G8) countries, which established an Africa Action Plan in 2002 to pledge funding and logistical support for African-led peacekeeping operations, support the idea of an ASF (ibid, p1-15).

It is in this new era of peacekeeping that South Africa has declared itself willing to contribute to peace operations under the auspices of the UN, AU, and the SADC. With no short-term solutions or 'quick fixes' for many of the conflicts on the continent, South Africa need to carefully choose which resources to deploy, where these resources are most required and which environment best reflects its national interests (Kent and Malan, 2003: 1-5).

Given the asymmetry in the region, the hegemonic nature of South Africa's economic position and the nature of African state collapse, the country and the region requires a new paradigm that can serve to motivate and frame the engagement of issues of good governance, corruption and democracy in a manner that does not directly threaten African leaders of long standing. In the process, the challenge for South Africa is to lead by example and not through dominance. It is an immense challenge, but one that the country must face, if it is to survive and eventually prosper (Cilliers, 1999:1-16).

Current doctrine acknowledges that while PSO will be supported by CIMIC, the prime responsibility for peace building rests with civilian agencies. The view is that the most cost-effective use of scarce resources can be achieved by the early development of a multi-agency strategy or mission plan. This should draw together the activities of the various agencies so as to achieve both unity of purpose and effort. This plan need to develop an entry strategy to co-ordinate the incremental engagement of various agencies into the mission and to define lines of operation, objectives, main effort, exit strategies and co-ordination mechanisms. It may well be that the main effort does not lie with the military.

2.3.3   **SECTION 4: CIVIL-MILITARY COORDINATION (CIMIC)**

The large number of multidimensional actors present in today's complex peace operations and the broad range of issues they deal with have made coordination among the various multifunctional actors a crucial element in the success of these missions (Standard Generic Training Module 10, 2003:1-14).

Coordination is needed among the various components of a UN peace operation, the UN mission and other international, bilateral and NGO components, local government/administration and the parties to the conflict. International and local multidimensional actors include the humanitarian relief community, the peace building and development community, military peacekeepers, civilian police and others involved in the criminal justice system, human rights organisations, election specialists and observers, as well as those responsible for conflict prevention and peacemaking (ibid, p.1-14).

The relationship between humanitarian and military activities and cooperation between those engaged in them occupies an important place in the current international debate on crisis management. Multidimensional peace-support operations may focus on tasks in the civilian and humanitarian domain. Such an extension could lead to potentially problematic relations and even competition between the military and humanitarian organisations (ibid, p.1-14).

More importantly, if the dividing line between humanitarian and military action is blurred, the very concept of humanitarian action are undermined. The simultaneous presence of humanitarian organisations in situations of armed conflict and mandated PE forces require a complementary, two-pronged approach: on the one hand, a contribution to the political resolution of the conflict that takes into account its underlying causes and on the other, the alleviation of the civilian population's suffering due to the crisis (Studer, 2001: 367-391).

Next, the learning programs of UNITAR POCI present a generic training program in which all peacekeepers around the globe could participate, to establish a sound basic knowledge of peace missions.

2.3.4 **SECTION 5: UNITAR POCI LEARNING PROGRAMS**

One of the most important purposes of the UN is "to maintain international peace and security to that end to take effective collective measures for the prevention and removal of threats." PK provides the UN with one of the means of achieving international peace and security. It has developed as a pragmatic response to problems requiring the UN actions (Standard Generic Training Module 1A, 2003: 1).

UNITAR POCI offers 18 different self-paced correspondence learning programs, all of which are available in English. Learners that enroll in these courses include commissioned military officers, non-commissioned officers, diplomats, NGO employees, humanitarian workers, teachers, civilian police, and ordinary citizens interested in peace.

After a learner has studied all lessons and finished the quizzes, he or she completes the 50-question multiple choices end-of-course examination provided with each program. Answers sheets are submitted to UNITAR POCI for grading. If learners achieve a passing grade of 75%, they are awarded a Certificate-of-Completion for that individual program. UNITAR POCI presents the following programs:

An Introduction to the UN System: Orientation for Serving on a UN Field Mission

Learners gain a solid introductory foundation in the workings and structure of the UN and UN initiatives to support peace. Topics include the task and mission organisation, the principal organs of the UN, the UN's role in maintaining peace and security, the UN's role in the fields of development and related humanitarian actions, the environments, principles of duties and responsibilities, safety and security, the available tools, and the institutional partners involved in peacekeeping (Hårleman, 2003: 1-185).

History of United Nations Peacekeeping Operations during the Cold War: 1945 to 1987

The program provides learners with an understanding of the genesis, origin, and evolution of UN Peacekeeping and the background of the UN Charter. It covers the Arab-Israeli conflict and peacekeeping missions in Korea, Lebanon, the Congo, India and Pakistan, the Middle East, Cyprus, and Africa. The program discusses military peacekeeping as a means to promote the peaceful settlement of disputes (Liu, 1999: 1-123).

History of United Nations Peacekeeping operations following the Cold War: 1988 to 1997

This course discusses the political and diplomatic background and the perspectives that shaped UN peacekeeping during a period when superpower rivalry ended and the community of nations sought to form a new world order, with UN peacekeeping playing a central role. It traces UN peacekeeping and peace enforcement during the years following the Cold War: The Persian Gulf, Yugoslavia, Somalia, Rwanda, Mozambique, Angola, Cambodia and Central America (Liu, 1998:5-195).

Peacekeeping in the Former Yugoslavia: From the Dayton Accord to Kosovo

Since the conclusion of the Cold War the United Nations have been called upon to intervene in more conflicts and keep the peace in more places than in the previous 45 years since the UN has been established. This expansion in the size, scope and complexity of PK operations has been exemplified by the events that occurred in the former Yugoslavia during the 1990s. The program familiarizes the learner with the military and political efforts to bring peace to the Former Yugoslavia 1995-1999. It discusses the historical background, the Dayton Accord, UN missions prior to IFOR, SFOR, NATO, The Kosovo Crisis, the KLA and the JLA, the role of the media, missions completed and ongoing. This theater of operations has been one of the UN's greatest challenges in the new realms of peace making, peace enforcement, peace building, as well as traditional and second generation PK operations. (Ram and Juyal, 1999: 1-278).

Global Terrorism

This learning program reflects the events of September 11, 2001 and emerging details of the global phenomenon of terrorism. Topics included are: origins of contemporary terrorism, domestic, international and transnational terrorism, guerilla warfare and the Geneva conventions, war crimes and crimes against humanity, terrorism and human rights violations, proclaimed motivations and justifications, profile, structure and practice of terrorist organisations, terrorist's weapons, improvised explosive devices (IED), nuclear, biological and chemical weapons, suicide terrorists, mutilation, ethnic cleansing, structure destruction, hijacking, kidnapping, hostages, nuclear terrorism, new religious terrorism, counter-terrorism, special police formations, Al Qa'ida attacks on the USA, UN resolutions and instruments against terrorism, political integrity and will to counter terrorism. The program also includes case studies, a glossary, extracts from security in the field, statistics of death, injury and hostage taking in UN missions, as well as a list of useful security and related publications (Medhurst, 2002:1-575).

Principles for the Conduct of Peace Support Operations

Peacekeepers need to be guided by deep understanding of UN organisations and principles. In order to operate in the mission efficiently and effectively, they should have a clear picture of the background, functions and, in particular, the role of the UN in PK activities.

The peacekeepers should also be capable of interoperating in a conflict or post-conflict area within a multinational and multidisciplinary environment, respectful of different cultures and professional ethics and able to avoid conflict-escalation while ready to cope with it (Standard Generic Training Module 1B, 2003:1).

Learners learn the operational applications and political implications of the full range of PSO's in today's complex environment. Conceptual approaches, principles, operational techniques, PK, PE, peace support, combat, the promotion of consent, and planning for peace operations (Wilkinson, 1996:1-191).

<u>The Conduct of Humanitarian Relief Operations</u>

Learners learn how humanitarian relief is provided to refugees and victims of war and natural disasters. Topics include a history of humanitarian relief, the development of humanitarian action in the 20th century, international humanitarian organizations, specialized government structures, NGOs, the Red Cross, principles of intervention, respect for at-risk populations including women and children, international humanitarian law, management of humanitarian emergencies, population security and safety, managing a refugee camp, community health care in humanitarian intervention, control of communicable diseases and epidemics, relief convoys, shelter, distribution of food aid, water management, collective sanitation, sustainable solutions to humanitarian crises, freely consented repatriation, asylum, conducting elections, establishment of civil institutions, the humanitarian charter, minimum standards for disaster relief, code of conduct in rescue and disaster situations (Conoir, 2002: 1-228).

73

Serving as a United Nations Military Observer: Methods and Techniques

The content of this course is consistent with the methods and practices of UN Peacekeeping that have been established over the past 50 years. Much of the material in this course is based on the UN military observers manual. The student should refer to appropriate policy documents and other authoritative sources when serving on a UN observer mission. How to serve as a UN military observer (MILOBS), dealing with culture shock and understanding social customs: MILOBS duties on patrols and observer posts, the code of conduct, impartiality, liaison, negotiation, communication and security are aspects dealt with (Hårleman, 1997: 1-169).

Security Measures for United Nations Peacekeepers

Peacekeepers are finding themselves in more diversified security environments than ever before. It is critical that all have a clear understanding of basic security awareness principles and responsibilities to ensure that they can effectively perform their duties. Considerations for security at the residence, while engaged in walking or jogging, preparation for travelling both internationally or internally in the country of assignment, what to do in the event of a breakdown, accident, ambush or car hijacking, are provided to better prepare the peacekeeper for the daily threats he/she may encounter (Standard Generic Training Module 06, 2003:1).

This program follows in the wake of September 2001. Although this learning program does not deal specifically with aviation security and national defence, its syllabus encompasses several aspects of security concerning terrorism, useful on the individual scale, especially for UN Peacekeepers and those deployed under field conditions, for which this course is purposely designed. This learning program prepares military and civilian personnel for inevitable security problems on any UN mission. Topics include security defined, security in UN missions, security in the mandate, HQ security, bases, checkpoints, vehicles, communications, weapons, defense, diplomatic and envoy status, assault, rape, hostage-taking, terrorist bombing, ambushes and blackmail. It also includes case studies, a glossary, field extracts, statistics of death and injury and hostage taking in UN missions (Medhurst, 2002: 1-247).

Peacekeeping and International Conflict Resolution

This program is aimed at anyone working in a zone of conflict. As such, the program may be useful to both military and civilian representatives of the international peacekeeping community. Given the complexity and diversity of contemporary conflicts, and the range of actors involved in trying to create and sustain peace in war-torn societies, it does not intend to provide the student with a prescription for resolving the world's conflicts. As no two conflicts are identical, effective conflict intervention requires understanding, flexibility and creativity. The program offers the learner a broad understanding of the fundamental concepts, principles and techniques of conflict resolution that may be applied in a variety of contexts and on a number of different levels. It seeks to provide the learner with some of the conceptual, analytical and practical tools that will allow him or her to understand and operate more effectively in peacekeeping environments (Woodhouse and Duffey, 2000:1-239).

Commanding United Nations Peacekeeping Operations

This course prepares commissioned officers and non-commissioned officers (NCOs) to lead their troops on peacekeeping operations. Students learn the military, institutional and legal background to PK. Organisation of command, methods of command, rules of engagement, principles, operational techniques, action and the use and non-use of deadly force is included in learning material. How peacekeepers conduct observation posts, patrols, convoys, escorts and refugee and humanitarian operations is briefly discussed. Support of diplomatic initiatives, prisoner exchanges, protecting civilians, dealing with parties in conflict and humanitarian agencies are conversed (Faure, 1996:1-165).

United Nations Civilian Police: Restoring Order Following Hostilities

Most experts agree that the role of the United Nations Civil Police (UN CIVPOL) is crucial to the success of post-Cold War peace operations. Working closely with military peacekeepers and observers, CIVPOL are a key resource in re-establishing a "rule of law" necessary for all other government institutions to function properly and for economic activity and "peace building" to take place. In order to execute this important job, CIVPOL observers must be trained. This program familiarises the learner with the roles and duties of UN CIVPOL in restoring civil order following chaos. Topics include the history of CIVPOL, privileges and immunities, cultural relations, staff duties and reporting, communications, safety, principles, liaison, negotiation and security (Forster, 1997:1-203).

<u>Mine Action: Humanitarian Impact, Technical Aspects and Global Initiative</u>

In this learning program the learner is introduced to the global problem of landmines and how international organisations are approaching the problem. The topics include The anti-personnel mine ban treaty (Ottawa MBT), mine action guidelines for ceasefires and peace agreements, landmine and unexploded ordnance (UXO) safety training, identifying landmines and UXOs, international mine action standards (IMAS) and guidelines for application, victim assistance, and mine risk education. Even when the hostilities of war are long past, these devices represent a lingering cruelty and an obstacle to recovery. It is this problem and cruelty that the authors of this program and others seek to confront. By studying the lessons of this program the learner will see what measures organisations and the international community are taking. The learner will also learn which contributions remain to be made (Donoghue and Wilkinson, 2003: 1-293).

<u>International Humanitarian Law and the Law of Armed Conflict</u>

This high level program covers international humanitarian law (IHL) as applied to soldiers, humanitarian workers, refugees, displaced persons and others involved with armed conflict. Topics include background and definitions, protection of victims, rights of prisoners of war, rules of conduct in hostilities, means of implementation, human rights and IHL, applicability of IHL to PK and PE, different applications to inter-national and intra-national conflicts, terrorism, sovereignty and the role of the International Red Cross (IRC) in IHL (Bouvier, 2000:1-187).

<u>Logistical Support to United Nations Peacekeeping Operations</u>

For the future peacekeepers working in their national environment in their mother country, logistics seldom creates problems. Serving in a UN mission may not be very different, but if the peacekeepers deploy to a mission just being established, they may face some hardships. All the facilities mentioned in their own country have to be established in the mission area and this is usually a shared responsibility between the UN and the troop contributing country (TCC). UN operations are rather complex with respect to logistic support. No two missions are the same, as the support to the UN from host nations, troop contributing countries and contractors differs (Standard Generic Training Module 15, 2003:1).

This learning program introduces students to logistics operations in UN peace operations. It gives the background and rationale behind UN PK logistics, the strategy employed in the field and at Headquarters (HQ), introduces the mission life-cycle, explains how financial support is gained and introduces the different components that make up integrated logistics support in a field mission (Baig, 2002:1-265).

<u>Operational Logistical Support of UN Peacekeeping Missions</u>

UN missions can vary in size from a small group of observers who may be civilians, police, military or a mixture, to a combined operation of land, sea and air forces involving tens of thousands of personnel. Consequently, various logistic concepts will need to be considered to fulfill a mission's logistic requirements.

This program provides the learner with a background in intermediate-level topics of UN operational logistics. Topics include an overview of UN operational logistics, command and control, planning, supply, engineering support, fire protection, environmental measures, transportation, aviation and air services, maintenance, medical aspects of logistical support, communications, as well as postal and courier services (Leslie, 1999: 1-201).

2.4   CONCLUSION

Peace and security issues have become priority issues, not only for the African continent, but also for the international community. The importance of the peace and security design is associated with a number of different factors. The creation of the AU must be seen as a step of crucial importance in the development of peace on the African continent.

In connection with some positive developments at regional level and with the NEPAD initiative, the AU is now seen as constituting a realistic "African reform program" designed to set new African political accents, and at the same time to consciously seek support from abroad.

The dynamics developed by African reform efforts have been accompanied by an altered outside perception of Africa's growing significance to international politics. Apart from the global security perspective, Africa is currently experiencing a geo-strategic renaissance. Some African regions are becoming important world oil suppliers. The USA, as well as other countries such as China, is increasingly coming to view parts of the continent from an angle of energy security.

Against the background of Africa's dynamics and new security agenda, external actors are adapting their instruments and rethinking their options. After a series of disappointing peace missions in the 1990s (particularly in Angola, Rwanda, Somalia and Liberia), the UN Security Council has begun to renew its peace efforts in Africa (Burundi, Cote d' Ivoire, Democratic Republic of the Congo and Liberia, for example).

Increasingly cross-cutting approaches are being sought that integrate elements from the fields of foreign policy, security and development policy. Interfaces and overlaps between civil and military spheres have grown at pace. The African continent has increasingly become the focal point of UN peacekeeping missions after the low ebb of the 1990s.

Peace missions call for a focus on comprehensive approaches, involving sufficient civil components (developmental peacekeeping) with the inherent challenge for sufficient post-conflict peace-building funding and capital.

The ownership and political leadership of external civil and military interventions must lie with African institutions. Although the AU's ownership approach to peace and security on the African continent is fundamentally correct, it is contradictory to the funding and implementation capacities that are available.

UN military missions, both small and large and under widely varying mandates, have been staffed by multinational peacekeeping forces composed mainly of military units and military personnel who have been trained through their own national programmes.

Although these missions require a large number of military specialists, the involvement of civilians has expanded significantly, particularly where a peacekeeping operation has been called upon to perform duties that are less military in nature.

The same tendency prevails in other areas of UN field operations such as the more peaceful development activities. All UN field missions require staffing by personnel with extensive professional training in their own field of expertise.

In addition, these staff members must have an awareness of the complex working environment, including political, economic, and social and security conditions in the field. They must also have knowledge of multidisciplinary structures, especially the UN system itself. Personnel have to acquire the ability to handle these intricate concerns. This requires a coherent and cohesive training system that covers training at all levels.

Self-paced correspondence courses, such as those of UNITAR POCI, should be regarded as part of such a system. It is primarily aimed at those who are or would like to become members of UN/AU field missions and who would like to become better familiarised with the UN, its system, working conditions and requirements in the field.

There is an emerging consensus on the need to prepare for coordination before conflicts arise. This preparation involves better training that gives the military an insight into the ways in which humanitarian workers operate and familiarises themselves with the military approach.

Knowing and respecting each other's mandates can help prevent misunderstandings. Training is, moreover, a means of fostering predictability. This is very important for the military, for which the world of humanitarian action is one of perplexing diversity.

Training in advance also provides an additional opportunity to spread knowledge of international humanitarian law and especially its particular implications for peace-keeping operations among national troops.

Knowledge of the UN Secretary-General's guidelines on international humanitarian law should be promoted, too, by the UN and by the governments themselves.

Military activity is but one element that has to integrate into the conduct of the overall campaign. The demands for comprehensive training are higher for peacekeeping operations than for war-fighting, particularly as the severity of extreme peace-support operations can equal, and even exceed, those of much war-fighting.

The diversity of tasks and sometimes their unexpected nature means that the training manuals cannot cope with every eventuality. This, in turn, implies that junior officers and NCOs may have to cope with situations drawing on inculcated values gained through education rather than procedures and tactics learned in training.

Education takes time and has to nurture. "Growing education" is a big concept and dependent on national education systems (Herrly, 2005: 1).

It is essential that personnel from all nations are guided by standard UN and AU approved operating procedures and that training is available to familiarise personnel with established doctrine. Such training must be standard, doctrinally correct, easily delivered to personnel of all nations, up-to-date and inexpensive.

Since the nature of PK on the African continent is comprehensive and complex, the importance of training is more evident, underscoring the urgent need for the AU to have a well-trained and prepared ASF participating in its various operations.

Since the attitudes, tactics and methods of peacekeeping operations diverge from conventional military doctrines, efforts must be taken to improve understanding of peacekeeping principles and techniques.

The proposed Model of Co-operative Education on PSO in Africa will assist in training peacekeepers by enhancing the general understanding of PK and providing specific knowledge of methods for serving on peace missions. The demands being made on PK and the multifaceted character of contemporary operations call for greater attention to be paid to the training and preparation of anyone involved in a PK operation.

CHAPTER 3 - RESEARCH DESIGN AND METHODOLOGY

3.1   INTRODUCTION

Chapter 3 documents the methods and procedures used to achieve the research objectives: to determine whether there is a need for a Model of Co-operative Education on PSO in Africa, to design a Model of Co-operative Education on PSO in Africa in accordance with scientific instructional design (ISD) principles and to draft curriculum content on PSO in accordance with the principles of curriculum design.

The chapter presents a discussion on the design of the study. It begins with an account of the sample that includes the sampling techniques employed and the criteria used in the choice of sample size. A description is given of the measuring instruments used to determine whether there is a need among military officers for PSO education and to analyse the possible target group that could participate in the program. Details of the data collection process that includes gaining access to the subjects, data collection techniques and the procedure used are reported on.

The rationale behind the selection of data analysis procedures, as well as the actual procedures used is described and possible sources of limitation in the quality of data collected are discussed.

3.2   **DESIGN OF THE STUDY**

Research defines as the search for and the generation of new knowledge through scholarly work (Bless & Higson-Smith, 1995:43). The overall plan followed is a non-experimental design. In a non-experimental design there is no manipulation of the independent variable, nor is the setting strictly controlled (SANDF COLET, 2003a:9).

Based on the four-dimensional framework, it becomes possible to categorise the study as one of an empirical nature using primary and secondary sources, as well as numerical and textual data type with medium control (Mouton, 2001:146).

The design report and curriculum are classified as applied research, as they form part of an original investigation undertaken with the primary aim to expand on fundamental knowledge and to apply it after completion (Lategan, Vermeulen & Truscott, and 2003:1). The research is generally descriptive by nature and its main advantage is immediate application after having obtained results. The instructional design (ISD) is "applying scientific knowledge about human learning to the practical tasks of teaching and learning." ISD technology translates and applies basic research (Newby et al., 2000:10).

Learning theory forms part of the descriptive sciences which describe the way in which things function in the natural world, while the ISD forms part of the design sciences which offer means in which to perform certain human-defined tasks. Descriptive sciences are the law, while design sciences are roadmaps and there is always more than one way to get from point A to point B (Clark, 2000:15).

In order to evaluate the programme content, the researcher will make use of a reputability study. This involves the researcher identifying experts from academic institutions. The comments and criticisms of these experts form the basis of the formative evaluation (Bless & Higson-Smith, 1995:50). The structure of this research design is a framework of clearly formulated decision steps as depicted in Figure 1.

Figure 1: Research Design Framework

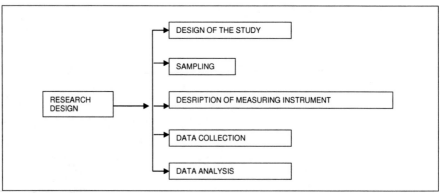

Source: Own

3.3   **SAMPLING**

The researcher has the responsibility of defining the population to be studied (Bless & Higson-Smith, 1995:85). The study included all officers in the SANDF (population), irrespective of rank, age or gender. However, in the light of the size and complexity of the SANDF, the respondents (target population) have been selected from the South African Army (SA Army).

The proposed units (sample frame) from which the respondents were drawn used probability cluster sampling, which included units in the SA Army. These units are representative of the mainstream of SANDF units and selected because they form part of the full time component, their members are utilised for force employment operations internally or externally and they are used for peace support operations under the auspices of the United Nations (UN) or African Union (AU).

The abovementioned reasons make the sample representative of the total population (SANDF). The results are generalised to the total population. A sample randomly drawn from the units of the SA Army reflects as closely as possible the characteristics of the entire population, although the selected sample can rarely, if ever, be a mirror image of the population. Representivity implies that the sample has the same properties as the population from which it was drawn, but in smaller numbers (Welman & Kruger, 1999:45).

All organisational levels were identified and included individual officers, irrespective of rank, age, gender, race or former force in order to ensure a representative sample. Criteria for inclusion in the sample required that participants had to be members of the armed forces, play an active role in the activities of their units, must have had at least two years of experience (in the case of officers) and the literacy level of respondents needed to include the ability to read, write and follow instructions. Subsequently, the population sample frame that completed the questionnaire consisted of 90 officers. According to Welman and Kruger (1999:50), no sample should be fewer than 15 units of analysis, but preferably more than 25.

In order to ensure that each member at a specific unit had an equal chance of selection, the researcher used simple random probability sampling (Corbett and Le Rog, 2003:104). Firstly, a name list of all the officers at the respective units identified all the units of analysis in the sampling frame. A numerical number was allocated to each participant. Secondly, the mechanism selected a table of random numbers that showed no order, irrespective of whether one proceeded along its columns or rows to choose the unit of analysis that ensured that each number had an equal chance of being selected. In other words, if one started at any given number, there was no way in predicting the value of the next number. Next, the numbers of the units of analysis (in the sampling frame) encountered on the table of random numbers were written down. The advantage of a simple random sample is that it was representative of the population in the sense that it did not favour one unit of analysis (individual) over another (Welman and Kruger, 1999:51). The questionnaires were numbered and distributed according to the selected units of analysis.

3.4   DESCRIPTION OF THE MEASURING INSTRUMENT

The measuring instrument, with consideration of the specific objectives of the research, was an attitudinal scale questionnaire comprising sets of items to determine the need for a higher learning programme, assisting in the analysis of the target group. Even though perceptions, attitudes, feelings or the reaction of men and women may have limits, Schneider, Asworth, Higgs, and Carr (1996: 695), noted that significant correlations exist between employee reports of the practices and procedures under which they work, as well as judgements made by external observers. This suggests that people are an accurate gauge of the influence of one variable on others.

According to Welman & Kruger (1999:150) the rationale for using a questionnaire by means of group contact is working with captive audiences that correspond to the administration of a test, since a single person is required to give instructions in one hall. The cost per questionnaire is lower and the supervisor is in full control of the completion of the questionnaires so that no respondent has an excuse not to complete his/her questionnaire.

Subsequently, a response rate of 100% is ensured. Due to the presence of a supervisor, queries regarding the completion of the questionnaire were answered immediately. Another reason for using a questionnaire is that it identifies and describes the characteristics of the sample (Welman & Kruger, 1999:164).

Advantages include the potential to generalise to large populations (Mouton, 2001:153). They are easily standardised, a low drain on time and finances and requires very little training of researchers (Bless & Higson-Smith, 1995:114). Disadvantages include a lack of depth and insider perspective that sometimes leads to criticism of "surface level" analysis (Mouton, 2001:153).

It is difficult to check that the respondent understands the questions (Bless & Higson-Smith, 1995:114). The respondent may choose not to answer a question or questions (questionnaires are therefore not always complete), he/she may guess the answers if uncertain (this may lead to inaccurate results) and cannot clarify any response provided by the respondent (SANDF College of Educational Technology, 2003:48).

3.5 **DATA COLLECTION PROCEDURE**

The theoretical framework that informed the study was a literature search and review based on the aim and research objectives of the study as presented in Chapters 1 and 2. The review is sufficiently comprehensive and used essential information sources. It offers a logically organised and integrated summary and theories relevant to the aim of the study. Primary data comprised of an attitude scale questionnaire to collect individual-level data.

Contact was made with the officers commanding of the applicable SA Army units to obtain authorisation and determine a suitable date, time, venue and contact person that will administer the completion of the questionnaire. The visitation programme and information with respect to the project included a description and layout of the nature and extent of the project, as well as an explanation of the procedure to complete the questionnaire. On the day of the survey, a questionnaire was handed to each respondent at the respective units as arranged and collected after completion on the same day.

A pilot study assessed the validity and reliability of the questionnaire, the correctness of some concepts, the adequacy of the method and the instrument of measurement (Bless & Higson-Smith, 1995:43). The participants in the pilot study consisted of 15 officers of the Air Defence Artillery School and 20 officers of the Army Support Base Kimberley.

The criteria for inclusion in the sample were that members had to be either combat participants, combat support participants or combat service support participants. They must have had at least two years of experience in the force and be willing to participate in PSO. The reason for including these respondents is that they belong to SANDF units and have an interest in operations other than war.

In designing the data-collection methods, the researcher concentrated on two important aspects that could have had a significant influence on the credibility and acceptability of the results. These two concepts are the reliability and validity of data-collection methods (SANDF College of Educational Technology, 2003:56). Effective questionnaire construction ensures measurement reliability and effective controls high construct validity (Mouton, 2001:153).

An ISD model formed the blueprint for the design of the proposed learning programme and curriculum. A model is an abstract of a real world situation, the entire process of analysing learning needs and outcomes and the development of a delivery system to meet the outcomes (Briggs, 1977:28).

The model assisted in providing a visual outline of the exact process that would follow. Singled out was the SANDF College of Educational Technology (COLET) basic model, as its design accommodates learning programme research and development requirements (SANDF College of Educational Technology, 2003b:12).

The model provides all essential activities, is scientifically justifiable, simple and logical, shows the relationship between the components and makes provision for a feedback system across the entire system. The process includes analysing qualifications, formulating outcomes, determining and sequencing content, determining the delivery methods, training material and activities, assessment, programme strategy and curriculum development.

The evaluation of the design report and curriculum entails a reputability study. This involved the Central University of Technology, Free State (CUT), identifying experts from within the community and academic institutions. Each expert received a draft copy of the design report, curriculum and a reaction sheet to complete. These experts voiced their opinions on the learning programme contents and the method of implementation. The comments and criticisms form the foundation of the summative evaluation (Bless and Higson-Smith, 1995:50).

ISD based on the principles of Educational Technology makes a significant contribution towards the improvement of training quality. It not only facilitates the implementation of a systems approach, but also places training on a scientific basis from where informed decisions are possible. Various models for instructional design share most of the common, basic components (Walkinshaw, 1992:13).

According to Van Dyk, Nel, Loedolff, and Haasbroek (2001:162), to be reliable and valid, a model needs to adhere to the following: Improve learning and instruction by means of the problem-solving and feedback characteristics of the systematic approach; Improve management of instructional design and development by means of monitoring and control functions of the systematic approach; Improve evaluation processes by means of the designated components and sequence of events, including the feedback and revision events inherent in models of systematic instructional design and test or build learning and instructional theory by means of a theory-based design within a model of instructional design.

3.6   DATA ANALYSIS

Statistical analysis is a method of rendering meaningful, quantitative information (SANDF College of Educational Technology, 2003a:62). After collecting data, an appropriate statistical method was selected to test the research question (Corbett and Le Rog, 2003:5).

The appropriate method for interpreting data was descriptive statistics as described by SPSS computer software (SPSS, 1999). Data recorded as numerical values enable the analysis thereof by statistical means.

Measurement took place on an ordinal level in order to rank data in terms of a formulated order. Descriptive frequencies are converted to percentages illustrating the levels of agreement. Statements accompany tables to describe the results.

During instructional design, the method for interpreting data inherent to the Plan, Develop, and Assess (PDA) model of systematic instructional design used assessment of the designated components and sequence of events, including feedback and revision events.

3.7.   LIMITATIONS OF THE STUDY

This research functions within the following limitations: An attitude scales questionnaire does not directly observe the behaviour of subjects, but individuals report on it in terms of the questions put to them. These measuring instruments are therefore susceptible to measurement reactivity, the consequences of which may vary from withholding co-operation to deliberate deception.

The participant's awareness that he/she is completing a measuring instrument may have affected his/her responses to the subsequent completion of the questionnaire. Participants might have responded in a manner not consistent with their true opinion, but what they think is the most suitable response or will portray them in a positive light. Dishonesty in surveys on the part of respondents is a problem (Corbett and Le Rog, 2003:111).

Respondents being biased may be possible due to biases introduced by unresponsive participants, uncooperative participants answering at random and also by those who give false information on purpose due to mistrust, fear, conformity or social status pressures. Furthermore, one can add answers based on the misunderstanding of a question or word or the difficulty experienced by respondents in expressing themselves.

The design and development of a learning programme require a considerable amount of funds for the procurement of books and other material, the development and production of instructional materials, the possible utilisation of consultants and printing costs.

The choice of instructional methods and strategies may be a constraint that requires consideration. As the fulltime availability of learners is in doubt, it restricts programme design options.

It is possible to underestimate the development of a new programme, especially if the design of the programme is subject to effective evaluation before implementation.

According to Langholtz, de Beer and Mostert (2003:11) problems may arise in extending the learning programme to other countries in Africa in support of the NEPAD initiative. Effective evaluation and refinement of the programme is therefore necessary before offering it to other African countries.

3.8   **CONCLUSION**

This chapter explained the methods and procedures that were used to achieve the research objectives. A non-experimental quantitative design expanded on concepts, ideas and constructs to answer the research questions. The approach considered scientific instructional design based on the principles of educational technology. The participants (target population) were selected from the SANDF. The measuring instrument with consideration of the objectives of the study was an attitudinal scale questionnaire.

The theoretical framework that informed the study was a literature review based on the aim and problem statement of the project. Primary data comprising of an attitudinal scale questionnaire were used to collect individual level data. The pilot study conducted indicated that no changes to the questionnaire were necessary. The members involved in the pilot study did not form part of the main study. The data analysis of the main survey was carried out by using the SPSS statistical package. It was also indicated that the starting point to the ISD process was an ISD model. Possible limitations were indicated.

The chapters that follow record the results of the study by the presentation and the interpretation of data and show the extent of ISD used to produce a design report and curriculum concerning a Model of Co-operative Education on PSO in Africa.

CHAPTER 4 - RESEARCH RESULTS

4.1 INTRODUCTION

This chapter is an account of the results of the study according to the research objectives, presented in the form of an ISD report. The reporting begins with Section 1 on Need Analysis, reflecting whether there is a need among SA Army officers in the SANDF for a Model of Co-operative Education on PSO in Africa. It also answers the question on the best method to design such a learning programme.

Section 2 presents a job description and target group analysis. The purpose of the job description was to establish generic job performance and to identify training needs from which learning outcomes will derive. The aim of the target group analysis is to create a learner profile that describes the characteristics of the target population.

The purpose of Section 3 was to align the generic job requirement of a peacekeeper with the training needs. The job requirement, the qualification and the unit standards are required to match. This, together with the information from the literature review, translates into exit outcomes and specific outcomes.

Sections 4, 5, 6 and 7 describe the development of ETD opportunities with reference to development, delivery and assessment.

4.2   **SECTION 1 – NEED ANALYSIS**

Chapter 1 established that there is a need for PSO education. No major university in South Africa is currently contributing towards education in the field of generic PSO in Africa. Broadening the knowledge and skills based through higher education is a means of shaping appropriate attitudes and setting the right expectations to help SANDF members and NGOs adapt to the demands of PSO.

The purpose of this section is to determine whether there is a need for a Model of Co-operative Education on PSO in Africa amongst officers of the SA Army and, if there is, how to design such a curriculum.

Van Dyk et al. (1992:164) articulate that a needs analysis has the purpose of assessing the unique requirements of a situation. According to Rothwell and Kazanas (1992:46), a needs assessment is a scheme for collecting information concerning ETD needs.

This section essentially focuses on the following critical questions and possible course considerations:

• Critical Question 1: Is there a need among SA Army officers in the SANDF for a Model of Co-operative Education on generic PSO in Africa?

• Critical Question 2: What is the best method to design such a learning programme?

97

4.2.1   **CRITICAL QUESTION 1:** IS THERE A NEED AMONG SA ARMY OFFICERS

IN THE SANDF FOR A MODEL OF CO-OPERATIVE EDUCATION ON

GENERIC PSO IN AFRICA?

4.2.1.1   Attitudinal survey. An attitudinal questionnaire assisted in establishing whether

there is a need for a model on co-operative education amongst officers of the SA

Army.

Table 1: Survey Results

Peace missions are multi-dimensional operations with a political, economical,
social, legal and security-related focus.

		Frequency	Percent	Valid Percent	Cumulative Percent
Valid	Strongly disagree	3	3.3	3.3	3.3
	Disagree	2	2.2	2.2	5.6
	Uncertain	9	10.0	10.0	15.6
	Agree	42	46.7	**46.7**	62.2
	Strongly agree	34	37.8	**37.8**	100.0
	Total	90	100.0	100.0	

The military is one of many role players in the processes in which civilians and
police officers have become essential to the success of PSO.

		Frequency	Percent	Valid Percent	Cumulative Percent
Valid	Strongly disagree	4	4.4	4.4	4.4
	Disagree	8	8.9	8.9	13.3
	Uncertain	6	6.7	6.7	20.0
	Agree	37	41.1	**41.1**	61.1
	Strongly agree	35	38.9	**38.9**	100.0
	Total	90	100.0	100.0	

The SANDF relies on general-purpose combat training supplemented by mission-specific training to prepare soldiers for peace missions.

		Frequency	Percent	Valid Percent	Cumulative Percent
Valid	Strongly disagree	4	4.4	4.4	4.4
	Disagree	4	4.4	4.4	8.9
	Uncertain	11	12.2	12.2	21.1
	Agree	55	61.1	**61.1**	82.2
	Strongly agree	16	17.8	**17.8**	100.0
	Total	90	100.0	100.0	

General-purpose training on its own is not adequate to equip military personnel with the full range of skills required to meet the challenges presented in African PSO.

		Frequency	Percent	Valid Percent	Cumulative Percent
Valid	Strongly disagree	1	1.1	1.1	1.1
	Disagree	13	14.4	14.4	15.6
	Uncertain	20	22.2	22.2	37.8
	Agree	33	36.7	**36.7**	74.4
	Strongly agree	23	25.6	**25.6**	100.0
	Total	90	100.0	100.0	

Training in non-combat skills is as important as general-purpose combat training if one is to succeed as a peacekeeper.

		Frequency	Percent	Valid Percent	Cumulative Percent
Valid	Strongly disagree	3	3.3	3.3	3.3
	Disagree	6	6.7	6.7	10.0
	Uncertain	9	10.0	10.0	20.0
	Agree	47	52.2	**52.2**	72.2
	Strongly agree	25	27.8	**27.8**	100.0
	Total	90	100.0	100.0	

I need more peacekeeping training and experience to do my job as a peacekeeper well.

		Frequency	Percent	Valid Percent	Cumulative Percent
Valid	Strongly disagree	4	4.4	4.4	4.4
	Disagree	3	3.3	3.3	7.8
	Uncertain	8	8.9	8.9	16.7
	Agree	40	44.4	**44.4**	61.1
	Strongly agree	35	38.9	**38.9**	100.0
	Total	90	100.0	100.0	

It is not necessary for all members of the SANDF to undergo formal training in PSO.

		Frequency	Percent	Valid Percent	Cumulative Percent
Valid	Strongly disagree	26	28.9	**28.9**	28.9
	Disagree	38	42.2	**42.2**	71.1
	Uncertain	8	8.9	8.9	80.0
	Agree	10	11.1	11.1	91.1
	Strongly agree	8	8.9	8.9	100.0
	Total	90	100.0	100.0	

Current SANDF courses on PSO are too short.

		Frequency	Percent	Valid Percent	Cumulative Percent
Valid	Strongly disagree	2	2.2	2.2	2.2
	Disagree	9	10.0	10.0	12.2
	Uncertain	43	47.8	47.8	60.0
	Agree	21	23.3	**23.3**	83.3
	Strongly agree	15	16.7	**16.7**	100.0
	Total	90	100.0	100.0	

There is sufficient time to put theory into practice.

		Frequency	Percent	Valid Percent	Cumulative Percent
Valid	Strongly disagree	4	4.4	**4.4**	4.4
	Disagree	30	33.3	**33.3**	37.8
	Uncertain	28	31.1	31.1	68.9
	Agree	22	24.4	24.4	93.3
	Strongly agree	6	6.7	6.7	100.0
	Total	90	100.0	100.0	

The PSO course content should be more in-depth.

		Frequency	Percent	Valid Percent	Cumulative Percent
Valid	Strongly disagree	1	1.1	1.1	1.1
	Disagree	9	10.0	10.0	11.1
	Uncertain	31	34.4	34.4	45.6
	Agree	32	35.6	**35.6**	81.1
	Strongly agree	17	18.9	**18.9**	100.0
	Total	90	100.0	100.0	

The PSO course content focuses too much on general-purpose combat training (conventional warfare).

		Frequency	Percent	Valid Percent	Cumulative Percent
Valid	Strongly disagree	1	1.1	1.1	1.1
	Disagree	14	15.6	15.6	16.7
	Uncertain	39	43.3	43.3	60.0
	Agree	27	30.0	**30.0**	90.0
	Strongly agree	9	10.0	**10.0**	100.0
	Total	90	100.0	100.0	

The variety of PSO courses in the SANDF is limited.

		Frequency	Percent	Valid Percent	Cumulative Percent
Valid	Strongly disagree	3	3.3	3.3	3.3
	Disagree	8	8.9	8.9	12.2
	Uncertain	34	37.8	37.8	50.0
	Agree	38	42.2	**42.2**	92.2
	Strongly agree	7	7.8	**7.8**	100.0
	Total	90	100.0	100.0	

Everybody has equal access to current PSO training.

		Frequency	Percent	Valid Percent	Cumulative Percent
Valid	Strongly disagree	16	17.8	**17.8**	17.8
	Disagree	28	31.1	**31.1**	48.9
	Uncertain	23	25.6	25.6	74.4
	Agree	18	20.0	20.0	94.4
	Strongly agree	5	5.6	5.6	100.0
	Total	90	100.0	100.0	

I enjoy attending long courses away from home (3 months and longer).

		Frequency	Percent	Valid Percent	Cumulative Percent
Valid	Strongly disagree	14	15.6	**15.6**	15.6
	Disagree	35	38.9	**38.9**	54.4
	Uncertain	10	11.1	11.1	65.6
	Agree	21	23.3	23.3	88.9
	Strongly agree	10	11.1	11.1	100.0
	Total	90	100.0	100.0	

I prefer training to take place at my local unit.

		Frequency	Percent	Valid Percent	Cumulative Percent
Valid	Strongly disagree	8	8.9	8.9	8.9
	Disagree	25	27.8	27.8	36.7
	Uncertain	10	11.1	11.1	47.8
	Agree	32	35.6	**35.6**	83.3
	Strongly agree	15	16.7	**16.7**	100.0
	Total	90	100.0	100.0	

Members will be more motivated to attend military courses if the courses are accredited at an external tertiary education institution.

		Frequency	Percent	Valid Percent	Cumulative Percent
Valid	Strongly disagree	4	4.4	4.4	4.4
	Disagree	6	6.7	6.7	11.1
	Uncertain	8	8.9	8.9	20.0
	Agree	33	36.7	**36.7**	56.7
	Strongly agree	39	43.3	**43.3**	100.0
	Total	90	100.0	100.0	

The SANDF does not need a culture of lifelong learning.

		Frequency	Percent	Valid Percent	Cumulative Percent
Valid	Strongly disagree	33	36.7	**36.7**	36.7
	Disagree	26	28.9	**28.9**	65.6
	Uncertain	12	13.3	13.3	78.9
	Agree	10	11.1	11.1	90.0
	Strongly agree	9	10.0	10.0	100.0
	Total	90	100.0	100.0	

Training enhances employee confidence.

		Frequency	Percent	Valid Percent	Cumulative Percent
Valid	Strongly disagree	1	1.1	1.1	1.1
	Disagree	4	4.4	4.4	5.6
	Uncertain	2	2.2	2.2	7.8
	Agree	35	38.9	**38.9**	46.7
	Strongly agree	48	53.3	**53.3**	100.0
	Total	90	100.0	100.0	

Officers and Warrant Officers will be more motivated to attend courses if the focus is on self-development.

		Frequency	Percent	Valid Percent	Cumulative Percent
Valid	Strongly disagree	2	2.2	2.2	2.2
	Disagree	2	2.2	2.2	4.4
	Uncertain	11	12.2	12.2	16.7
	Agree	41	45.6	**45.6**	62.2
	Strongly agree	34	37.8	**37.8**	100.0
	Total	90	100.0	100.0	

All Warrant Officers and Officers in the SANDF should have the opportunity to obtain a relevant tertiary qualification.

		Frequency	Percent	Valid Percent	Cumulative Percent
Valid	Strongly disagree	1	1.1	1.1	1.1
	Disagree	2	2.2	2.2	3.3
	Uncertain	5	5.6	5.6	8.9
	Agree	33	36.7	**36.7**	45.6
	Strongly agree	49	54.4	**54.4**	100.0
	Total	90	100.0	100.0	

I would attend a United Nations accredited national diploma/degree course on PSO if granted the opportunity.

		Frequency	Percent	Valid Percent	Cumulative Percent
Valid	Strongly disagree	1	1.1	1.1	1.1
	Disagree	2	2.2	2.2	3.3
	Uncertain	9	10.0	10.0	13.3
	Agree	25	27.8	**27.8**	41.1
	Strongly agree	53	58.9	**58.9**	100.0
	Total	90	100.0	100.0	

A national diploma/degree on PSO will allow us to create a competitive advantage in developing new knowledge and skills for the future.

		Frequency	Percent	Valid Percent	Cumulative Percent
Valid	Strongly disagree	1	1.1	1.1	1.1
	Disagree	2	2.2	2.2	3.3
	Uncertain	4	4.4	4.4	7.8
	Agree	33	36.7	**36.7**	44.4
	Strongly agree	50	55.6	**55.6**	100.0
	Total	90	100.0	100.0	

Correspondence instruction with regular contact sessions is a good idea.

		Frequency	Percent	Valid Percent	Cumulative Percent
Valid	Strongly disagree	3	3.3	3.3	3.3
	Disagree	3	3.3	3.3	6.7
	Uncertain	7	7.8	7.8	14.4
	Agree	38	42.2	**42.2**	56.7
	Strongly agree	39	43.3	**43.3**	100.0
	Total	90	100.0	100.0	

A national diploma/degree qualification will assist officers and warrant officers towards a new career after retrenchment or early pension.

		Frequency	Percent	Valid Percent	Cumulative Percent
Valid	Strongly disagree	1	1.1	1.1	1.1
	Disagree	2	2.2	2.2	3.3
	Uncertain	5	5.6	5.6	8.9
	Agree	33	36.7	**36.7**	45.6
	Strongly agree	49	54.4	**54.4**	100.0
	Total	90	100.0	100.0	

4.2.1.2   Data Interpretation and findings of the survey indicate the following:

There is broad consensus among officers of the SA Army that the SANDF relies on general-purpose combat training (GPCT), supplemented by mission specific PSO training to prepare for peace missions (80% agree/strongly agree).

Members agree/strongly agree that GPCT on its own is not adequate to equip military personnel with the full range of skills required to meet the challenges present in African PSO (79%).

SA Army officers is of the opinion that training in non-combat skills is as important as GPCT if one is to succeed as a peacekeeper (80% agree/strongly agree).

The majority of SA Army officers felt that there is a need for more peacekeeping training and experience to execute their jobs as peacekeepers effectively (83.3% agree/strongly agree).

Seventy one percent (71%) of the respondents strongly agree/agree that it is necessary for all members of the SANDF to undergo peacekeeping training.

More than half of the respondents, 55% agree or strongly agree that PSO courses should be in more depth.

The respondents believe that members will be motivated to attend additional training if a tertiary institution accredits such training (80% strongly agree/agree).

A large number of the SA Army officers (65.6%) participating in the survey is of the opinion that the SANDF needs a culture of lifelong learning.

The vast majority (92%) of SA Army officers agree/strongly agree that training enhances confidence.

Respondents agree or strongly agree (91%) that all warrant officers and officers in the SANDF should get the opportunity to obtain a relevant tertiary qualification.

The large numbers of 86.7% agree or strongly agree that they would attend a UN accredited, national diploma/degree course in PSO.

Results indicate clearly that a national diploma/degree in PSO will allow the SANDF to create a competitive advantage in developing new knowledge and skills for the future (92.3% agree/strongly agree).

Respondents indicate that correspondence instruction with regular contact sessions is a good idea to present a learning program such as PSO (85.5% agree/strongly agree).

The attitude of 91% (agree/strongly agree) of SA Army officers is that a national diploma/degree qualification will assist them and warrant officers in starting a new career after leaving the defence force.

4.2.1.3   Summary

The results of the survey confirm that a performance problem exists. The survey results are a very strong indicator of the attitude of SA Army officer in the SANDF towards PSO training and higher education on PSO.

The results of the survey confirm that there is an unambiguous need for a Model of Co-operative Education on PSO in Africa among SA Army officers in the SANDF.

ETD cannot be planned in isolation or according to own standards. The design of a learning programme must take place within the context of the ETD environment as it has developed and exists today. Legislation such as national standards and qualifications, unit standards, outcomes-based education and training and relevant role-players govern outcomes (SANDF COLET, 2003b:67).

Although there are existing courses presented by UNITAR POCI, other international institutions and defence forces, it is important that African doctrine for PSO should not only derive from abroad. African realities are inevitably different from the environment that has shaped European and American doctrinal development.

A deduction is that the learner target group will not be available on a full time basis. The probable learning approach is correspondence instruction or first generation distance education supported with second-generation distance education, which includes limited face-to-face co-operative education supported with distance education modes of delivery such as e-learning (CF. Badenhorst, 2004). This multimode method offers flexible in-service training of peacekeeping militia all over the world, in essence, the co-operative training model per excellence.

Distance education is most effective when used to reach a large population of geographically distributed learners who require standard training in knowledge-based topics and when the training must be delivered directly to learners without delay and at a low per-learner cost. (Langholtz, de Beer, and Mostert, 2003:11).

However, not all the factors that could influence this solution are available and therefore a final decision with regard to programme approach is not yet possible.

4.2.2   **CRITICAL QUESTION 2: WHAT IS THE BEST METHOD TO DESIGN A LEARNING PROGRAM?**

Achieving concurrence with international and national obligations and needs became important when South Africa joined international organisations, of which the most significant are the UN, AU and the SADC. The resulting involvement in multi-national peace PSO on the African continent provides the direction for ETD requirements at different levels.

The need to transform the education and training approach in South Africa reflects in the Constitution of the RSA, Act 108 of 1996, deciding on an outcomes-based education (OBE) and training approach (SANDF COLET, 2006:1).

The National Qualifications Framework (NQF) is the RSA's answer to global and national demands for a change in the approach to ETD, promulgating an ETD system, which is learner-centred and will encourage learners to accept responsibility for their own learning (van der Westhuizen, 1998:29).

The South African Qualifications Authority (SAQA) (Act 85 0f 1995), states that the purpose of all ETD is to equip learners with KSAs that will enable meaningful participation in society. The National Skills Development Strategy, the Skills Development Act (Act 97 of 1998) and the DOD Human Resource (HR) 2010 Strategy compel the SA DOD to enable its employees to transfer KSAs to meaningful civilian careers outside the SANDF (DOD Strategy 2010, DoD: White Paper, 1998:23; National Skills Strategy; Skills Development Act 97 of 1998).

The SA DOD recognises that it is necessary to establish ETD standards that promote approval, excellence, recognition and accreditation (De Vries, 1997: 33). The future goal is to educate, train and develop decision-makers in the SA DOD who are "fit for the challenges of the 21st century" (Modise, 1997:2). Van Dyk, Nel and Loedolff (1992:147) define education as activities aimed at developing knowledge, moral values and understanding required in all aspects of life. According to Jerling, (1999:3) education is a comprehensive concept and may even include the concepts of training and development. Erasmus and Van Dyk (1999:2) define training as a systematic and planned process to change the

KSAs of employees in order to achieve organisational objectives. Van Dyk et al. (2001: 148) define training as a systematic process of changing the behaviour and/or attitudes of people in a certain direction to increase goal achievement within the organisation. Zemke (1999:8) states that training is about giving people the knowledge and skills to do their jobs.

De Cenzo and Robbins (1994:255) suggest that development focuses on future jobs in the organisation. Development refers to possibilities within a job, with reference to the employee's personal growth and goals (Nel, Gerber, Van Dyk, H. Schultz, and Sono, 2001:49). Development aims to empower employees serving in a managerial capacity or preparing for managerial posts within the organisation (Van Dyk et al. 2001:148), referring to learning opportunities designed to help individuals grow (Bernadin and Russell, 1993:297).

It is essential to see the concepts of education, training and development in relation to one another if both the organisation and employees are to benefit. Education is essential for every individual, both for life in general and the workplace in particular. Training and development will succeed only if the individual has received an adequate standard of education. Training is necessary to correct work procedures and improve performance at the workplace. Development, on the other hand, should enrich not only the individual, but also the group. From this, it is clear that these concepts are interrelated (Zwane, 1995 in Jerling 1999:3).

SAQA accepted OBE as the prescribed system for all education and training programmes, which require accreditation in terms of the NQF (Van Dyk et al. 2001:150). OBE implies that everything focuses on what is essential for the learner to be able to do at the end of the learning experience (Spady, 1994:2).

According to SANDF COLET (2006:2), OBE is as an approach, which focuses on the outcomes of learning, with the emphasis on what the learner should be able to do.

The concept of educational technology (Ed Tech) has become increasingly important in the field of ETD. Technology is the systematic application of scientific or other related knowledge to practical tasks (Galbraith, 1967: 12), concerned with teaching (Knirk and Gustafson, 1986:16), applying scientific knowledge regarding human learning to teaching and learning (Heinrich, Molenda, Russell, and Smaldino, 1993:16).

Definitions that is more recent states Ed Tech is the theory and practice of design, development and evaluation of processes and resources of learning (Seels, 1995:1) or the use of knowledge, systems and techniques to enhance human learning. It is a broader applied discipline within the broader science of education. Essential characteristics of Ed Tech are that it supports a systems approach, continuous evaluation and learning programmes designed according to instructional design (Van der Walt, 2005: V).

So, why use ISD to create a learning programme? Simply stated, ISD is a common sense approach to ETD. It analyses the problem, designs a specification, develops the courseware, implements the solution and performs evaluations throughout the process (Clark 2000:1).

ISD is a means of planning a learning programme from the point of need analysis until the presentation of the programme. It is a process to create effective training in an efficient manner (SANDF COLET, 2003b:2) and to translate principles of learning into plans for learning activities and materials (Smith and Ragan, 1999:2).

Newby, Stepich, Lehman, and Russell (2000:67) has a similar view by describing ISD as a systematic process for developing plans for instruction through practical application of theoretical principles.

4.2.2.1   Point of Departure

ETD that occurs within an organisation typically has one main purpose, the improvement of organisation effectiveness (Langenbach, 1993:11). The ETD process is self-sustaining, continuously improved and updated, based on the feedback fed into the process. The ETD process (see figure 2) is the point of departure for the design of this learning programme, further enhanced through an ISD model (SANDF COLET, 2003b:11).

Figure 2: ETD process

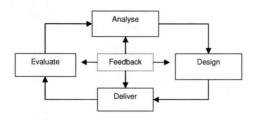

Source: Adapted form SANDF COLET, 2003b:18

A variety of ISD models related to the ETD process explains how the ETD processes apply in different situations (Jerling, 1999:70). Dick and Carey (1996:4) emphasise that there is no single approach for designing instruction. The various models, however, all share the same basic components. Models are very useful, as they enhance the chances of success in training design (Van Dyk et al. 2001:162). The intention was not to describe each of the following models in any detail, but rather to concentrate on the main activities of the ISD process in general. The models examined included the high-impact model (Chang, 1994:15), Nadler's critical events model (Nadler, 1982:12), the model of Camp, Blanchard and Huszco (Camp et al, 1986:4), the outcomes-based curriculum design (Olivier, 1998:44), generic competency-based training model (Blank, 1982:26), literacy curriculum model of Newman (Langenbach, 1993:82) and the COLET basic model (SANDF COLET, 2003b:14). The various model's all share the same basic components (Van Dyk et al., 2001:162) illustrated in figure 3 (Bramley, 1991:6). The situation within each organisation determines the model of choice.

Figure 3: The main elements of ISD

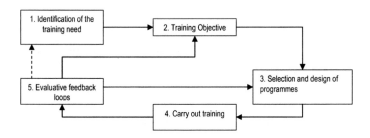

Source: Bramley 1991:6

A customised model named Plan, Develop and Assess (PDA) incorporates the various elements of training design for the design of this learning programme. The PDA model meets the terms of an instructional design model as it does the following:

- Adjusts to the SANDF's training system and training approach.
- Provides for all the essential activities.
- Is scientifically justifiable.
- Is simple and logic.
- Clearly indicates the mutual relationship between the components.
- Makes provision for a feedback system across the entire system.
- Is suitable for the particular situation.

The model has a built-in validity check and openness in the form of the evaluation and feedback loop that forms part of each event in the model. The model has definite inputs and outputs and the following main steps: plan, develop and assess. The PDA model consists of the components illustrated in figure 4 and applies as follows:

- All the steps of the models' planning component are utilised in the design of the learning programme.
- Use all the steps of the models development component during planning for the further development of the programme.
- The application of two steps of the models assessment component is relevant to the final report namely planning assessment criteria and reputability study.

Figure 4: PDA Model of Instructional Design

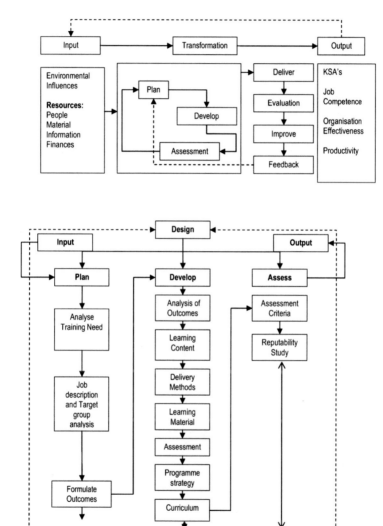

Source: Newby et al. 2000:8

115

A simple map of the model as illustrated guides the design of the learning programme. Figure 5 shows integration of the PDA model into ETD process.

Figure 5: ISD Model integration

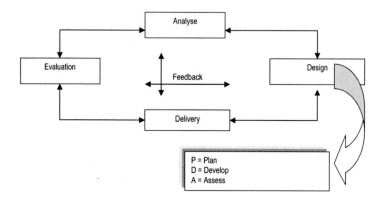

Source: Own

4.2.2.2 <u>Summary</u>

The purpose of this section was threefold: to confirm whether there is a problem with regard to training, to consider broad course options, to determine whether there is a need for a Model of Co-operative Education on PSO in Africa and to indicate how to design the envisaged programme. The technique used to collect information for the establishment of the training need was an attitudinal survey. The survey results indicate a training gap and confirm the need amongst SA Army officers in the SANDF to participate in a tertiary programme on PSO in Africa. The next section presents a job description and target group analysis.

4.3   **SECTION 2: JOB DESCRIPTION AND TARGET GROUP ANALYSIS**

4.3.1   <u>**INTRODUCTION**</u>

Section 1 established that there is a training need among SA Army officers in the SADF to participate in a Model of Co-operative Education on PSO in Africa. The section also made a declaration of departure point by identifying a model of ISD to assist in the compilation of the design report and curriculum.

The purpose of section 2 is to carry out a job analysis and analyse the target group for which the proposed Model of Co-operative Education on PSO in Africa is designed. The purpose of the job analysis is to establish generic job performance and identify training needs from which learning outcomes will be derived. The aim of the target group analysis is to create a learner profile that describes the characteristics of the target population for whom the training programme is designed.

If a training programme has to provide a worthwhile return on investment, it must be relative to the job. This means that the learning experiences provided for the learners during the training must be directly related to the duties and tasks they have to perform in the job situation. Consequently, it is essential that the job performance requirements, including accurate and objective job data, are gathered and analysed. Accurate training needs can be determined from job performance requirements (Van Dyk et al. 2001:191). Nadler (1982:47) maintains that, to specify job performance data, it is necessary to separate the person from the job and merely concentrate on the job.

4.3.2   **JOB DESCRIPTION**

Introduction

A comprehensive job description consists out of a job and task analysis, providing the trainer with useful information. Job analysis discover what tasks need to be performed in order to do the job and therefore, what needs to be learned in order to perform effectively (Bramley, 1991:11) in the process of collecting, tabulating, grouping, analysing, interpreting and reporting data pertaining to the work performed by individuals (Tracy, 1984:88). Erasmus and Van Dyk (1999:199) add that job analysis deals with the identification of various tasks and the knowledge, skills, abilities and responsibilities that a person must have in order to perform the job.

Task analysis is the process of breaking down a task into smaller units and then sequencing these units in order of priority based on their importance in performing the job (Carnevale, Gainer, and Meltzer., 1990:44), providing a comprehensive description of the task (Wolmarans and Eksteen, 1987:102). A job description, therefore, comprises of a list of functions and tasks within a particular job (Van Dyk et al. 2001:192).

Tracy (1984:91) states that regardless of how well the subsequent steps in instructional design, development and validation are carried out, if job data is not complete, valid and reliable, the resulting system will fail to produce personnel who are capable of performing their duties at an acceptable level of proficiency.

The method used in this section includes a combination of methods such as the questionnaire, the walk-and-talk technique and the analysis of PSO manuals.

Generic Job Description of a Peacekeeper

- The officer in a peacekeeping role must be able to serve on a UN or AU peacekeeping missions as a field operator in various positions such as military observer, liaison officer, staff officer, and commanding officer. Execute as part of a contingent, different types of peace operations in accordance with regulations and procedures.

- The officer must be able to plan, integrate (organise), direct and control the activities of human and other resources allocated to him/her.

- He/she guides work operations through the establishment of objectives, application of policies, rules, practices, methods and standards in order to prepare and ensure that elements under command is mission ready.

- He/she needs to promote a sense of intelligence/security awareness amongst subordinates. Collect, analyse, organise and critically assess any information relevant to peacekeeping missions in Africa to make a sound judgement of any given situation.

- Ensure a high standard of training with regard to different types of peace operations. Satisfy the need for tertiary education, improved knowledge and changed attitudes towards peace missions in Africa. Assess peacekeeping operations from an international perspective in order to apply lessons learnt in the African peacekeeping environment.

- Accept the responsibility for logistic planning, equipment, stores and buildings under control. Monitor the financial planning and control expenditure of allocated funds.

- Apply the elements of a geo-political study in order to compile a geo-political profile of a given country in Africa for peacekeeping purposes.

- Contribute to the CIMIC process by working in close collaboration with local authorities, UN peacekeeping forces and other agencies in ensuring safe access to vulnerable populations of concern.

- Ensure the essential dialogue and interaction between agencies and military actors that are required to protect, promote and ensure that humanitarian principles are applied and humanitarian operational goals achieved and, in doing so, any inconsistency in the pursuit of appropriate common goals is de-conflicted and/or minimised.

- Advocate that peacekeeping forces apply the "Law of Armed Conflict" (LOAC) and facilitate awareness training. Display the attitudes required to become an unbiased diplomat under the African Union or United Nations flag for peacekeeping operations.

- Be able to act as military observer and report on activities in his/her sector of operations. The officer has to maintain impartiality and objectivity in his/her dealings.

- The officer needs to be fluent in written and spoken English, physically fit, not HIV positive, of sound mental character, mature in attitude and outlook and equipped with the appropriate qualifications and experience for the mission. He/she must be in possession of a Code 8 driver's licence.

4.3.3   **TARGET GROUP ANALYSIS**

Training design places the learner central in the learning process (Walkinshaw, 1992:14). Therefore, a description of the learner group designated to participate in the learning program is important to determine entry requirements and decide on instructional methods, media, and techniques and approaches most appropriate (Van Dyk et al. 2001:178).

The results obtained from the survey questionnaire reflect in table 2 and form the basis for the description and analysis of the target group.

Table 2: Target group analysis survey results

Gender

		Frequency	Percent	Valid Percent	Cumulative Percent
Valid	Male	81	90.0	90.0	90.0
	Female	9	10.0	10.0	100.0
	Total	90	100.0	100.0	

Rank Group

		Frequency	Percent	Valid Percent	Cumulative Percent
Valid	Lt Col	9	10.0	10.0	10.0
	Major	33	36.7	36.7	46.7
	Captain	24	26.7	26.7	73.3
	Lieutenant	16	17.8	17.8	91.1
	Warrant-Officer	8	8.9	8.9	100.0
	Total	90	100.0	100.0	

Age

		Frequency	Percent	Valid Percent	Cumulative Percent
Valid	24 and younger	1	1.1	1.1	1.1
	25 and older	89	98.9	98.9	100.0
	Total	90	100.0	100.0	

Academic Qualification

		Frequency	Percent	Valid Percent	Cumulative Percent
Valid	Grade 10	3	3.3	3.3	3.3
	Grade 12	67	74.4	74.4	77.8
	Certificate	5	5.6	5.6	83.3
	Diploma	8	8.9	8.9	92.2
	Degree	7	7.8	7.8	100.0
	Total	90	100.0	100.0	

Language

		Frequency	Percent	Valid Percent	Cumulative Percent
Valid	English	43	47.8	47.8	47.8
	Afrikaans	42	46.7	46.7	94.4
	African Language	5	5.6	5.6	100.0
	Total	90	100.0	100.0	

Experience

		Frequency	Percent	Valid Percent	Cumulative Percent
Valid	0-5 years	2	2.2	2.2	2.2
	6-10 years	36	40.0	40.0	42.2
	11-15 years	25	27.8	27.8	70.0
	16-20 years	18	20.0	20.0	90.0
	21-30 years	9	10.0	10.0	100.0
	Total	90	100.0	100.0	

Learning Style

		Frequency	Percent	Valid Percent	Cumulative Percent
Valid	Activist	21	23.3	23.3	23.3
	Reflector	11	12.2	12.2	35.6
	Theorist	19	21.1	21.1	56.7
	Pragmatist	39	43.3	43.3	100.0
	Total	90	100.0	100.0	

Cultural Factor

		Frequency	Percent	Valid Percent	Cumulative Percent
Valid	Own community culture	13	14.4	14.4	14.4
	Military culture	46	51.1	51.1	65.6
	Functional group	5	5.6	5.6	71.1
	National culture	26	28.9	28.9	100.0
	Total	90	100.0	100.0	

Peace support operations course

		Frequency	Percent	Valid Percent	Cumulative Percent
Valid	Yes	32	35.6	35.6	35.6
	No	58	64.4	64.4	100.0
	Total	90	100.0	100.0	

Peace support operations deployment

		Frequency	Percent	Valid Percent	Cumulative Percent
Valid	Yes	21	23.3	23.3	23.3
	No	69	76.7	76.7	100.0
	Total	90	100.0	100.0	

4.3.3.1 Target Group Description and Analysis

A target group description gives an account of the characteristics that members of the target group have in common, i.e. "as is", whereas the analysis obtain information that could be valuable when specifically developing the learning programme and how it will influence the learning programme (SANDF COLET, 2004:6). Using the data obtained from the survey the following target group description and analysis was possible using the criteria biographical, background information and attitude:

Biographical Information

Culture. All are South Africans coming from diverse backgrounds. The largest percentage, 51%, views the military culture as the most important, whereas 28.9% prefers national culture.

The relationship between the different ethnic groups will vary in accordance with the degree in which their religious beliefs, values, language and customs correlate. Difference in mother tongue is frequently associated with ethnic differences; this could possibly lead to problems in a diverse group. Insufficient communication on the levels of training, administration and operational experience can lead to a lesser amount of effectiveness. Different attitudes and values characterise various ethnic groups. These attitudes and values form part of the education of the individual and form the basis for his/her outlook on life. These differences have an influence on the receptiveness of training, as well as the skill to perform normal daily military tasks and activities. It is therefore very important that all learners train in cross–cultural aspects and facilitators are sensitive towards issues of diversity. A strong a-political stance is necessary. Fortunately, the majority of respondents (51%) view the military culture as most important.

The language of respondents includes English, Afrikaans, and various African languages.

Language is not only a vehicle for communication; it is also a symbol of national and ethnic alliance. Problems could therefore arise in the selection of a language programme. One could avoid this by selecting a language that is not exclusive to any ethnic grouping. The survey results indicate that the majority of respondents prefer English as their language of choice; therefore, the thread language for the learning program will be English. Members can understand, write, read and communicate in English. This will enhance the effectiveness of communication. Forty eight percent (48%) of the members that participated in the survey prefer English as the common language.

Age. All the officers and warrant offices included in the survey were over the age of 25 years, i.e. the average age of the learner group is between 25 and 60 years.

Learners are all adults and able to follow a routine and adhere to discipline. Adults have a need to learn, are motivated, participate actively in the learning process and take responsibility for learning. The average age of the learners is 35 years. Most of the members are in their mid-career. Normally this is a time of success and major achievement. Members are therefore eager to learn as much as they can in order to advance their careers. According to Robbins (2001:33-36), age has no influence on productivity and therefore we conclude that no prospective members on this learning programme should have trouble with added responsibility. Older workers and those with longer tenure are less likely to resign.

Gender. Eighty-one (81) male and nine (9) female officers completed the survey.

The researcher assumes that gender should not have a significant impact on the program. According to Robbins (2001: 33-36), few differences affect performance between men and women. However, preferences for work schedules differ – working mothers prefer part-time work, flexible work schedules and telecommuting in order to accommodate family responsibilities. It might be difficult for them to attend anticipate contact sessions. In the case of absence and turn over rates, evidence is mixed.

Service years of the participants in the SANDF range from one to 30 years. Results indicate that the majority of members (77%) have between 6 and 15 years of experience in the military.

A wide variety of experience could compliment learning. Robbins (2001:33-36) says tenure has consistently related negatively to turnover. It is one of the single best predictors of turnover. Survey results indicate that the majority of respondents have between 6 and 15 years of service and therefore fall in a very stable category concerning turnover.

Rank group: Warrant officer to Lieutenant Colonel. Approximately 63% are in the rank group Captain to Major.

This indicates that officers that took part in the survey are senior members with experience of the military culture, values and norms. These members are able to take responsibility for their own learning. They have mutual respect for one another; and different learning experiences form a rich source of information.

Mustering: All the respondents are from the military, coming from different service components within the SA Army. The majority of members (82%) are from the teeth arms of the SA Army and includes infantry, armour, artillery, air defence artillery, intelligence and field engineers.

This means that all understand the use of military terminology and acronym examples. Most share a common culture in the military. All members of the

SANDF have done general-purpose combat training and therefore have a solid foundation as a starting point to convert into unbiased peacekeepers. All members have common organisational outcomes, and teamwork is established.

Physical Disabilities. None of the respondents has physical disabilities. Therefore, there is need for any special arrangements. A peacekeeper working in the field of physical PSO needs to fit according to military standards.

The marital Status of the group is either married or single. Marital status should not have a direct impact on the programme. There are not enough studies to draw any conclusions regarding the effect of marital status on productivity. However, Robbins (2001:33-36)) remarks that married employees have fewer absences, less turnover and report higher job satisfaction than unmarried employees do.

Background Information

Academic and Formal Qualifications. The majority (74.4%) has grade 12. Twenty-two and five percent (22.5%) has tertiary qualifications.

This means that all respondents are literate i.e. can read, write and comprehend information. They are able to identify and solve problems, carry out information processing and have an understanding of systems. Therefore, they will be able to organise themselves and their activities.

Military Qualifications. Military qualifications range from senior Non-commissioned officer (NCO) programs to junior command and staff duties program. All members have completed basic training, individual specialised training, sub-unit and unit training, integrated training and a wide array of other general-purpose combat training. The researcher concludes that a wide range of military experience gives the opportunity to use the existing competencies among members to the benefit of learning in the PSO field.

Previous experience relating to the topic of PSO. The majority of respondents (64.4%) have not completed a course in PSO. Of the respondents, 76.7% have not yet deployed as peacekeepers.

The results of the survey show that some members have deployed externally without having completed a formal peacekeeping course, indicating that there is a performance gap. The researcher reaffirms that the SANDF generally relies on general-purpose combat training with pre-deployment peace training to prepare its soldiers for peacekeeping missions.

Learner's Attitude

Learning style preferences common to this group include; Pragmatist 43%, Activist 23.3% and Theorist 21.1%.

This result means that the learning program needs to cater for all learning styles, especially during contact sessions. Pragmatists, the majority, would prefer practical exercises such as coaching and demonstrations. Activists would like to participate in competitive work and role-play exercises, whereas Reflectors would rather prefer to work individually, listen to a formal lecture or watch a video. Theorists would like to solve complex problems and conduct research.

Other learner attitudes such as what motivates them, what are their prime interests, what will hinder learning, an awareness of the advantages of attending the learning programme, whether forced or voluntarily and what they expect to gain from the learning event is not possible to obtain until the specific learner group enrols for the program. A questionnaire prior to the commencement of the programme will obtain this information.

Learner Profile

A learner profile is a narrative description of the target population that sets forth assumptions made about individuals who will likely participate in the learning program (Jerling, 1999:37). Table 4 is a narrative of the learner profile that is most likely to enrol for a learning program on PSO in Africa.

Table 3: Learner Profile

Prerequisite Knowledge, Skills and Attitudes		Other learner-related characteristics	
Previously learned Knowledge	Grade 12 qualification. Must have completed basic training, individual specialised training, sub-unit and unit training, integrated training and a wide array of other general-purpose combat training.	Experience	Only officers and warrant offices were included in the survey. Very diverse, i.e. includes all racial groupings, both male and female. Respondents are married and single. The average age of the learner group is between the 25 and 50 years. All respondents are from the military, coming from different service components within the SA Army. The majority of members (82%) are from the teeth arms of the SA Army and includes infantry, armour, artillery, air defence artillery, and intelligence and field engineers. Ranks are from Warrant Officer to Lt Col. Approximately 63% are in the rank group Captain to Major and have between 1 and 30 years experience. The majority of members (77%) have between 6 and 15 years experience in the military.
Previously learned Skills	Management Capability. The ability to use various types of weapons and other war fighting equipment. Speak English, Afrikaans and various African languages. 48% of the members that participated in the survey prefer English as the common language.	Aptitude	General supervision and appraisal. Authorising work of others. Technical advice and guidance. Responsibility towards budget. Responsible for equipment. Responsible for buildings.
Previously	All are South Africans coming	Attitude	Pragmatists, the majority, would

Prerequisite Knowledge, Skills and Attitudes		Other learner-related characteristics
learned Attitudes	from diverse backgrounds. The largest percentage, 51%, views the military culture as the most important, whereas 28.9% prefer national culture. Positive towards being a military practitioner. Attitude towards learning is Pragmatist 43%, Activist 23.3%, Theorist 21.1% and Reflector 12%.	prefer practical exercises such as coaching and demonstrations. Activists would like to participate in competitive work and role-play exercises, whereas Theorists would like to solve complex problems and conduct research. Reflectors would rather prefer to work individually, listen to a formal lecture or watch a video.

4.3.4   **SUMMARY**

This section dealt with the job description of the peacekeeper and target group analysis of the group surveyed. The purpose of the job analysis was to establish generic job performance. Emphasis was placed on a description of the target group and establishing the learner profile. The technique used to collect information for the target group analysis was an attitudinal survey. This resulted in a detailed description of the learner group expected to attend a possible learning program on PSO in Africa. The next section uses the job description to determine training needs and formulate learning outcomes.

4.4   **SECTION 3: THE FORMULATION OF OUTCOMES**

4.4.1   **INTRODUCTION**

In the previous sections the situation, job performance and target group was analysed. It is now possible to design the proposed program to be in line with the outcomes stated in the anticipated qualification and unit standards. Aligning the learning program with the qualification or part of the qualification enables the learner to receive credits for the qualification. It will allow the providers of training to align the delivery of their programs in a manner that will facilitate the learning result to transfer into a national qualification or part thereof. The qualification also addresses organisational needs. Alignment is necessary in order to comply with legislation and to train for impact. The generic job description of a peacekeeper, the information from the target group analysis, the learner profile, and the information from the literature review, translates into exit level outcomes and specific outcomes for the proposed Model of Co-operative Education on PSO in Africa.

4.4.2   **EXIT LEVEL OUTCOMES (OVERALL OUTCOMES)**

On completion of this qualification, the learner will be able to:

- Serve on UN peacekeeping missions in various positions such as military observer, liaison officer, and CIMIC officer.

- Assess peacekeeping operations from an international perspective in order to apply lessons learnt in the African peacekeeping environment.

- Appraise the elements of a geo-political study in order to compile a geo-political profile of a given country in Africa for peacekeeping purposes.

- Collect, analyse, organise and critically assess any information relevant to peacekeeping missions in Africa and to make a sound judgement of any given situation.

- Contribute to the CIMIC process by working in close collaboration with local authorities, UN peacekeeping force, and other agencies in ensuring safe access to vulnerable populations of concern.

4.4.3   **SPECIFIC OUTCOMES**

Serving on a UN Peacekeeping Mission:

- Assess the UN system and the mission environment.
- Assess the history of UN peacekeeping operations during the Cold War: 1945 to 1987.
- Assess the history of UN peacekeeping operations following the Cold War: 1988 to 1997.
- Assess peacekeeping in the former Yugoslavia from the Dayton Accord to Kosovo.
- Assess global terrorism.
- Assess international humanitarian law and the law of armed conflict.
- Assess security for UN peacekeepers.
- Assess the principles for the conduct of PSO.
- Assess peacekeeping and international conflict resolution.
- Appraise UN civilian police: restoring civil order following hostilities.
- Assess the conduct of humanitarian relief operations and principles of intervention and management.
- Assess operational logistical support of UN peacekeeping missions.
- Assess the provision of troops and contingent-owned equipment (COE) and the method for reimbursement.
- Assess UN military observers: methods and techniques for serving on a UN observer mission.
- Assess mine action: humanitarian impact, technical aspects and global initiatives.

- Appraise commanding United Nations peacekeeping operations.

Peacekeeping Operations from an International Perspective:

- Assess the strategic background to peace support operations.

- Assess the international environment.

- Assess the changing nature of peace support operations: A UK perspective.

- Estimate planning for peace support operations from a UK perspective.

- Value the general approach to peace operations (Netherlands).

- Compare the military approach to peace operations from a Netherlands perspective.

- Judge political decision-making and military command and control from a Netherlands perspective.

- Appraise support in a multinational framework from a Netherlands perspective.

- Value MOOTW operational tasks from a Netherlands perspective.

- Assess MOOTW from A USA perspective.

- Value the Principles of MOOTW, a USA perspective.

- Compare the types of MOOTW from a USA perspective.

- Estimate planning for MOOTW, a USA perspective.

- Judge hostage survival from a Canadian perspective.

- Appraise the operations centre from a Canadian perspective.

- Assess negotiation and mediation from a Canadian perspective.

- Value media awareness from a Canadian perspective.

- Value peace partners from a Canadian perspective.

- Assess preventive medicine (Canada).

- Assess stress management.

Geo-politics and Security studies:

- Appraise the concepts influencing Geo-Politics.

- Assess the elements of a Geo-Political study.

- Argue international politics.

- Assess Africa studies.

- Compare geo-politics: South Africa and SADC.

- Analyse global conflict.

- Assess international, regional and national security.

- Support world health issues.

- Value security-sector reform (SSR) in developing countries.

Peacekeeping Missions in Africa:

- Assess case studies in the African environment.

- Appraise the context in which PSO's take place.

- Discuss the strategic context and concepts of PSO in Africa.

- Appraise the fundamentals, principles and campaigning wrt PSO in the African context.

- Assess the tasks and techniques on PSO in the Africa context.

- Compare the components in PSO.

- Appraise the PSO environment.

- Estimate disarmament, demobilisation, and reintegration (DDR).

- Assess conflict analysis for project management.

- Estimate demobilisation and reintegration of ex-combatants in post-war and transition countries.

Civil-Military Coordination (CIMIC):

- Judge CIMIC relations principles.
- Appraise CIMIC in context.
- Assess CIMIC practices and processes.
- Value the military on humanitarian operations.
- Judge CIMIC individual skills.
- Set-up CIMIC exercises.
- Select options for aid in conflict.

4.4.4 CURRICULUM DESIGN FRAMEWORK

Outcomes identified above translate into the following possible learning programs:

Figure 6: Curriculum framework[1]

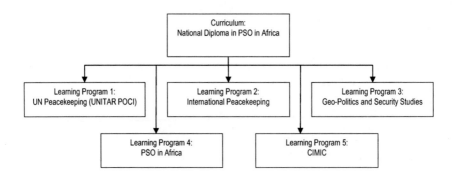

Source: Own

4.4.5 SUMMARY

This section formulated outcomes for the proposed Model of Co-operative Education on PSO in Africa. The training need identified by configuration with the job description and the literature review translated into exit level outcomes and specific outcomes for the proposed learning programs. The next sections attempts to develop ETD opportunities.

---

[1] Discussed with the Director: Curriculum Design, Unit for Academic development, Central University of Technology, Free State. Prof G. Mahlomosholo, Bloemfontein, 2006-06-12

4.5   SECTION 4: SELECTION AND SEQUENCING OF CONTENTU

4.5.1   **INTRODUCTION**

In this section a decision is made on the content required to achieve the outcomes and how it can be broken down into smaller steps to assist the learner. All the activities and the content are then sequenced. Content refers to the subject matter, teaching points and learning activities that will enable the learner to perform the various tasks and duties associated with the job of peacekeeping.

4.5.2   **SELECTION OF LEARNING CONTENT**

Table 4: Selection of Learning Content

Sn	Outcomes	Content
UNITAR POCI 1	An introduction to the UN system: orientation for serving on a UN field mission.	• The purpose and principles of the UN, its system and institutional framework. • The UN's roles in the areas of peace, security and development. • The applications of international humanitarian law and human rights. • The application of communication, negotiation and mediation technique. • The UN's role in maintaining safety and security • The general obligations and responsibilities of the Field Operator.
UNITAR POCI 2	The History of United Nations peacekeeping operations during the Cold War: 1945 to 1987.	• The history of UN Peacekeeping operations during the Cold War period 1945 to 1987. • The Arab-Israeli Conflict. • The first UN Emergency Force (UNEF). • The UN Operation in the Congo (ONUC)). • The financial crisis of the early 1960's. • West New Guinea (West Iran), Yemen and the Dominican Republic. • The UN Observation Group in Lebanon, India and Pakistan. • The second UN Emergency Force (UNEF II) and the disengagement UN Observer Force (UNDOF). • The UN Peacekeeping force in CYPRUS (UNFICYP). • The UN interim force in Lebanon (UNIFIL).
UNITAR POCI 3	The History of United Nations peacekeeping operations following the Cold War: 1988	• The end of the Cold War and the Resurgence of UN peacekeeping operations. • The UN Transition Assistance Group (UNTAG). • The Gulf Crisis and the use of force. • Further expansion of UN peacekeeping operations in 1991-1994

Sn	Outcomes	Content
	to 1997.	and New Challenges. • The performance of UN peacekeeping operations established In 1991-1994: The successful operations. • The performance of UN peacekeeping operations established In 1991-1994: The unsuccessful operations. • The second UN operation in Somalia. • The UN Protection Force in Yugoslavia. • The lessons from the UN operations in Somalia and Bosnia. • The Retrenchment of UN peacekeeping operations since 1994. • The situation of peacekeeping operations and future prospects.
UNITAR POCI 4	Peacekeeping in the former Yugoslavia: from the Dayton accord to Kosovo	• The Dayton accord. • UN/NATO operations prior to IFOR • IFOR (Implementation Force) • SFOR (Stabilization Force). • The role of the media. • The Kosovo Crisis: The Kosovo Liberation Army (KLA) and the Yugoslav Army (JA). • The Kosovo Crisis: NATO's role. • The ongoing missions in the former Yugoslavia in 1999. • The UN missions completed in the former Yugoslavia between 1995 and 1998.
UNITAR POCI 5	Global terrorism.	• The phenomenon of terrorism. • The definitions, elements and anomalies of terrorism. • The jjustifications proclaimed by terrorists. • Other motivations for terrorism: catalysts and negotiations. • The profile of terrorists and their organisations. • Terrorist weapons, resources and equipment. • The types of terrorist acts. • Terrorist tactics and the targets of terrorism. • The victims of terrorism. • Terrorism and the Cold War and terrorism and the media. • Anti-terrorism and counter-terrorism. • Terrorism, the United Nations and the Future.
UNITAR POCI 6	International Humanitarian Law and the Law of Armed Conflict.	• The general introduction to International Humanitarian Law (IHL): definitions and fields of application. • The protection of victims of International Armed Conflict. • Rules applicable in Non-International Armed Conflicts. • The rules on the Conduct of Hostilities. • The means of Implementing IHL. • Human rights law and International humanitarian law. • The applicability of international humanitarian law to peacekeeping and peace-enforcement forces. • The current role of the International Committee of the Red Cross (ICRC) in IHL.
UNITAR POCI 7	Security for UN Peacekeepers.	• Security in general. • Security in UN peacekeeping missions. • Security assets. • Military operational security. • Off duty security. • Security of urban buildings. • Threat recognition and minimising risk. • Treatment of victims.

Sn	Outcomes	Content
		• Mission (field) service; preparations & deployment. • Case studies.
UNITAR POCI 8	Principles for the conduct of peace support operations (PSO).	• Introduction to United Nations PSOs. • Conceptual approaches to PSOs. • Operational tasks. • The principles of PSOs. • Operational techniques. • Planning for PSOs. • Functions in combat. • Campaign planning.
UNITAR POCI 9	Peacekeeping and international conflict resolution.	• Overview of the emergence and development of the field of conflict resolution. • The nature of conflict. • The key concepts of conflict resolution • Contemporary conflict dynamics. • Conflict mapping. • Early warning and conflict prevention. • Peacekeeping and conflict resolution in war-zones. • Peace settlements and post-conflict peace building. • Culture, conflict resolution and peacekeeping. • Gender issues in peacekeeping.
UNITAR POCI 10	UN Civilian Police: Restoring order following hostilities.	• The history of CIVPOL operations. • The institutional framework and the universal principles established to restore international peace. • The essential parts of the preparation and conduct of negotiations and mediations. • The staff requirements of a peacekeeping operation and provide guidelines for writing various types of reports. • The UN communications systems and its international mandate. • The specific points regarding the security measures taken during a peacekeeping operation. • The administrative and logistic matters related to CIVPOL observers. • The first aid principles a CIVPOL observer should master and the health precautions that he or she should take before and during his/her service in a UN peacekeeping operation. • Specifics of what is required of a UN driver and the special terrain and weather conditions that he/she may meet in unusual climates. • Guideline organisation for United Nations Civilian Police. • The UN criminal justice standards for peacekeeping police.
UNITAR POCI 11	The Conduct of Humanitarian Relief Operations: Principles of Intervention and Management.	• The reasons for humanitarian intervention. • The actors in humanitarian relief. • The principles of intervention. • The management of humanitarian emergencies. • The management of health questions in humanitarian intervention. • Logistics: convoys, storage and distribution of aid and the management of shelters. • The administration of food aid. • Water management and sanitation. • Sustainable solutions to humanitarian crisis. • The principles of the "sphere" project and the "code of conduct".

Sn	Outcomes	Content
UNITAR POCI 12	Logistical Support to UN Peacekeeping Operations.	• The UN Peacekeeping Logistics Concept. • The organisation of the logistics support establishment both in the field and at headquarters. • The financial and budgetary aspects of peacekeeping logistics support. • The life cycle of a UN peace operation. • How peacekeeping field operations work with non-DPKO elements, both UN and non-UN. • The UNs' duties and responsibilities toward nations contributing troops and equipment to a peacekeeping mission. • The drawdown/liquidation process in a field mission.
UNITAR POCI 13	Operational logistical support of UN peacekeeping missions: intermediate logistics course.	• Overview of UN operational logistics. • UN operational logistic planning. • Supply concepts, supply planning and supply operations. • Engineering support. • The UN transportation system. • Aviation and air services. • The UN maintenance system. • The UN medical system. • The UN communications system. • The UN postal and courier services.
UNITAR POCI 14	The provision of troops and contingent-owned equipment (COE) and the method for reimbursement.	• The evolution of troop and contingent-owned equipment reimbursement. • The standard elements of the COE System and Lease Options. • The standards, verification and control on which the COE system is based. • Procedures and regulations governing the preparation and transportation of equipment to and from a mission as a part of a COE agreement. • Procedures for negotiating rates for specialized equipment that cannot be categorised into a generic group. • The responsibilities and procedures related to the loss and damage of equipment and supplies provided under the COE Agreement. • The purpose and calculation of mission factors as part of the COE reimbursement process. • The actual rates used to calculate reimbursement for major equipment. • Personnel-based self-sustainment rates. • How COE Agreements are prepared, approved and managed.
UNITAR POCI 15	United Nations military observers: methods and techniques for serving on a UN observer mission.	• The general outline of the UN system and enumerates specific details regarding some of the main components responsible for peacekeeping. • An in-depth review of the duties of the UN military observer and how he or she should present himself or herself to others. • The essential parts of the preparation and conduct of negotiations and mediations. • The staff requirements of a peacekeeping operation and provide a few guidelines for writing various types of reports. • The UN communications systems and its international mandate. • Some specific points regarding the security measures taken during a peacekeeping operation. • The administrative and logistic matters related to military

Sn	Outcomes	Content
		observers.
		• The first aid principles a military observer should master and the health precautions that he or she should take before and during the peacekeeping operation.
		• Specifics of what is required of a UN driver and the special terrain and weather conditions that he/she may meet in unusual climates.
UNITAR POCI 16	Mine Action: Humanitarian impact, technical aspects and global initiatives.	• The global landmine problem and UN response.
		• The anti-personnel mine ban treaty.
		• Landmine and unexploded ordnance (UXO) safety training.
		• International mine action standards (IMAS).
		• Victim assistance.
		• Mine risk education.
		• Mine information.
UNITAR POCI 17	Commanding UN PK operations using methods and techniques for PK on the ground.	• The institutional framework of PK operations.
		• The legal framework for PK operations.
		• The organisation and command for PK operations.
		• The organisation of force support within a PK operation.
		• The background of a PK operation.
		• The principles of action within a PK operation.
		• Domains and modes of action of the force.
		• Mission and operational techniques in PK operations
		• Specific techniques in PK operations
		• The rules of engagement in a PK operation.
		• Recommendations related to safety and security.
		• Rules of behaviour.
INTPSO	PSO from an international perspective	• The strategic background to PSO.
		• The international environment.
		• The changing nature of peace support operations: A UK perspective.
		• Planning for PSO's from a UK perspective.
		• The general approach to peace operations from a Netherlands perspective.
		• The military approach to peace operations from a Netherlands perspective.
		• Political decision-making and military command and control from a Netherlands perspective.
		• Support in a Multinational Framework from a Netherlands perspective.
		• PK operational tasks from a Netherlands perspective.
		• MOOTW from a USA perspective.
		• The principles of MOOTW, a USA perspective.
		• The types of MOOTW from a USA perspective.
		• Planning for MOOTW, a USA perspective.
		• Hostage survival from a Canadian perspective.
		• The operations centre from a Canadian perspective.
		• Negotiation and mediation from a Canadian perspective.
		• Media awareness from a Canadian perspective.
		• Peace partners from a Canadian perspective.
		• Preventive medicine (Canada).
		• Stress management.
AFRIPSO	PK missions in the African context	• Case studies in the African environment.
		• The context in which PSO take place.

Sn	Outcomes	Content
		• The strategic context and concepts of PSO in Africa. • The fundamentals, principles and campaigning wrt PSO in the African context. • The tasks and techniques on PSO in the Africa context. • Components in PSO. • The PSO environment. • Disarmament, demobilisation and reintegration (DDR). • Conflict analysis for project management. • Demobilisation and reintegration of ex-combatants in post-war and transition countries.
GEOPOL	Geo-political and security studies	• The concepts influencing geo-politics. • The elements of a geo-political study. • International Politics. • Africa Studies. • Geo-politics: South Africa and SADC. • Global conflict. • International, regional and national security. • World health issues. • Security-sector reform in developing countries.
CIMIC	Civil-military coordination (CIMIC) process.	• CIMIC principles. • CIMIC in context. • CIMIC practices and processes. • The military on humanitarian operations. • CIMIC individual skills. • CIMIC exercises. • Options for aid in conflict.

4.5.3   **SEQUENCE CONTENT**

Somehow you have to organise what you are going to do and when (Wilson, 1995:87). Sequencing is the process by which the content and learning experiences are organised to facilitate the maximum learning in the shortest time (Jerling, 1999:118) and to place content in the specific order in which it will be presented (SANDF COLET, 2003:102). The technique used in this paper is logical reasoning from general to specific (Rothwell and Kazanas, 1998:194), where the learner is first given a general overview of the topic and then introduced to more specific content. The leaner is therefore first presented with the broader picture before the specifics are taught.

Figure 7 depicts a proposed sequence of learning programmes and learning units, using a program map including alternative routes through the program (Wills, 1998:66).

Figure 7: Sequence of Learning Programmes

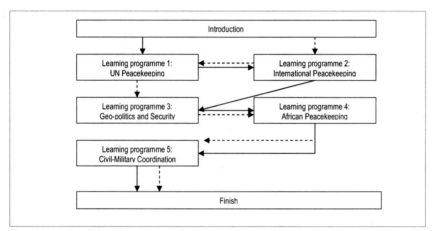

Source: Wills 1998:66

Table 5: Sequence of learning units

UN PEACEKEEPING (UNITAR POCI PROGRAMS)
An introduction to the UN System: Orientation for serving on a UN Field Mission
The history of UN peacekeeping operations during the Cold War: 1945 To 1987.
The history of UN peacekeeping operations following the Cold War: 1988 To 1997.
Peacekeeping in the former Yugoslavia: from the Dayton Accord to Kosovo.
Global terrorism
International humanitarian law and the law of armed conflict
Security for UN peacekeepers
Principles for the conduct of PSO.
PK and international conflict resolution
UN Civilian Police: restoring civil order following hostilities
The conduct of humanitarian relief operations: principles of intervention and management.
Logistical support to UN peacekeeping operations
Operational logistical support of UN peacekeeping missions: Intermediate Logistics Course
The provision of troops and contingent-owned equipment (COE) and the method for reimbursement
UN Military Observers: methods and techniques for serving on a UN observer mission
Mine action: humanitarian impact, technical aspects and global initiatives
Commanding UN peacekeeping operations: methods and techniques for PK on the ground

INTERNATIONAL PEACEKEEPING
Strategic background to PSO.
The international environment.
The changing nature of PSO: A UK Perspective.
Planning for PSO from a UK Perspective.
A general approach to peace operations (Netherlands).
A military approach to peace operations from a Netherlands perspective.
Political decision-making and military command and control from a Netherlands perspective
Support in a multinational framework from a Netherlands perspective
PK operational tasks from a Netherlands perspective
An introduction to MOOTW from a USA perspective
Principles of MOOTW, a USA perspective
Types of MOOTW from a USA perspective
Planning for MOOTW, a USA perspective
Hostage survival from a Canadian perspective
The operations centre from a Canadian perspective
Negotiation and mediation from a Canadian perspective
Media awareness from a Canadian perspective
Peace partners from a Canadian perspective
Preventive medicine (Canada)
Stress management

CIVIL-MILITARY COORDINATION (CIMIC)
CIMIC principles
CIMIC in context
CIMIC practices and processes
The military on humanitarian operations
CIMIC individual skills
CIMIC exercises
Options for aid in conflict

GEO-POLITICS AND SECURITY STUDIES
Concepts influencing geo-politics
Elements of a geo-political Study
International politics
Africa studies
Geo-politics : South Africa and SADC
Global conflict
International, regional and national security
World health issues
Security-sector reform in developing countries

PEACEKEEPING IN THE AFRICAN CONTEXT
Case studies in the African environment
The context in which PSO take place
The strategic context and concepts of PSO in Africa
The fundamentals, principles and campaigning wrt PSO in the African context
The tasks and techniques on PSO in the Africa context
Components in PSO
The PSO environment
Disarmament, demobilisation and reintegration (DDR)

4.5.4 **SUMMARY**

This section decided on the content required to achieve the outcomes and how it can be broken down into smaller steps to assist the learner. Content was sequenced to be placed in the specific order in which it will be presented. The next section will decide on the delivery method, training material and activities for the delivery of the learning programmes and curriculum.

4.6 **SECTION 5: DETERMINE DELIVERY METHOD, AND LEARNING AIDS**

4.6.1 **INTRODUCTION**

Rothwell and Kazanas (1998:210) define instructional strategy as an overall plan governing instructional content. Tracy (1984:244) uses the term strategy to describe all those activities employed in order to achieve a learning outcome, methods of delivery and learning aids.

A delivery method is the means by which instruction is offered (Rothwell and Sredi, 1992:10), a basic approach to instruction (Tracy, 1984:245). There is a large number of delivery strategies from which the designer of training can select (Van Dyk et al. 2001:249), cooperative education, competency-based, discovery, problem solving, games, simulation, discussion, drill and practice, tutorial, demonstration, presentation (Newby et al., 2000:91), computer-based, one-to-one, self-study, large scale presentation, small group and intact work group and correspondence instruction, for example (SANDF COLET, 2003b:111).

One cannot use instructional methods without also using some form of media for communication; printed material, computer software, slides, video, audio and multimedia, for example (Newby et al., 2000:100).

Media, according to Tracy (1984:245) include printed, projected and three dimensional aids and devices. It is not intended to cover the entire range of strategies, but merely to concentrate on the instructional strategies, methods and learning aids that can be used in the selection of an appropriate strategy.

4.6.2   **SELECTION OF DELIVERY METHOD**

In this section the final decision on the most suitable delivery method for the proposed learning programmes is made. In selecting a suitable method of delivery, Van Niekerk (1991b:74) considers the following factors: the nature of the outcome, the target group, content, time and other considerations.

Nature of the Outcome

The nature of the outcome that the learner must achieve is an important consideration in the selection of a delivery method (Van Niekerk, 1991b: 74). According to van Dyk et al. (2001:248) it is the overriding factor in the selection of delivery strategy. For this reason Tracy (1984:246) considers it necessary to examine the learning outcomes to establish the kind of learning involved. The following diagram assisted in the consideration of this factor.

Figure 8: Selection of delivery method according to nature of the outcome

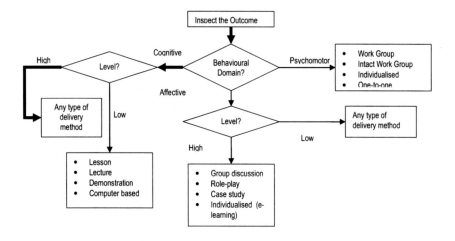

Source: Van Niekerk 1991: 75

The Target Group

The learner is a further factor to consider in the selection of method (Van Dyk et al, 2001: 248). Aspects such as age, grade level, socio-economic status, previous experience, what specific knowledge and skills they have, learning styles and preferences need to be considered (Newby et al., 2000:118). The influence of the learner group (level of maturity and previous learning experience) is accounted in figure 9.

147

Figure 9: Selection of delivery method according to target group

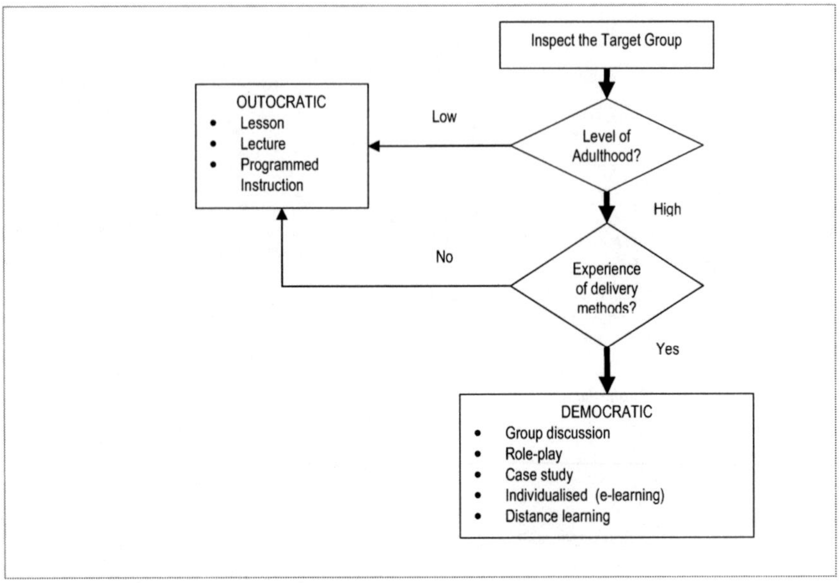

Source: Van Niekerk 1991:76

Content

The ability of the learner to master the content is another factor that has an influence on the selection of the delivery method (van Niekerk, 1991: 74). According to Tracy (1984: 246) the difficulty level of the programme content might influence the selection of a learning strategy. The diagram in Figure 10 indicates this influence.

Figure 10: Selection of delivery method according to content

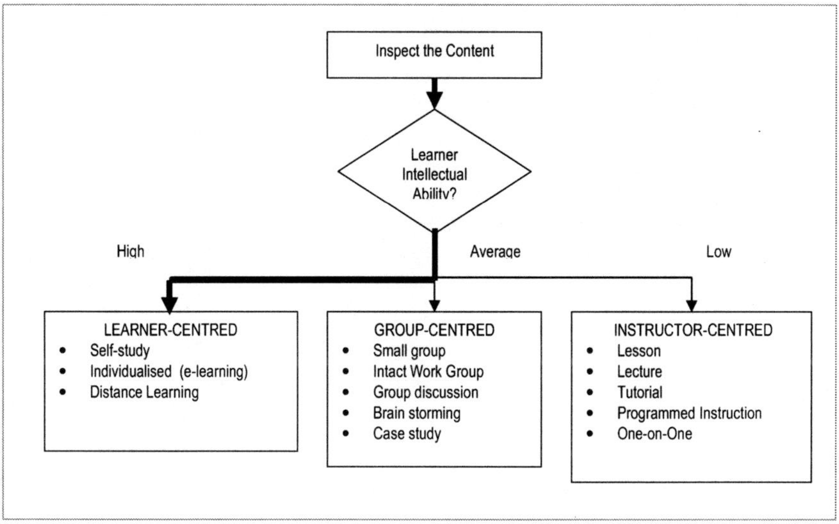

Inspect the Content

Learner
Intellectual
Abilitv?

High   Average   Low

LEARNER-CENTRED	GROUP-CENTRED	INSTRUCTOR-CENTRED
• Self-study	• Small group	• Lesson
• Individualised (e-learning)	• Intact Work Group	• Lecture
• Distance Learning	• Group discussion	• Tutorial
	• Brain storming	• Programmed Instruction
	• Case study	• One-on-One

Source: Van Niekerk 1991: 77

<u>Time availability of Learners</u>

The time availability for learning a particular subject or module may dictate the use of certain strategies (Van Dyk et al. 2001:177). Figure 11 assisted in the consideration of a solution.

Figure 11: Availability of learners

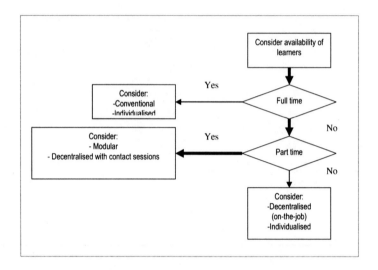

Source: Van Niekerk, 1991:75

<u>Other Considerations</u>

Policies and Procedures

It is not possible to plan and undertake ETD in isolation, nor according to one's own standards. Legislation such as national standards and qualifications, unit standards, OBE and training, and relevant role-players govern outcomes (SANDF COLET, 2003b:67).

Lecturers and Learners

The design and development of a meaningful and cost-effective learning programme require the utilisation of capable personnel who should not only be specialists in the field of peace support operations, but also be knowledgeable in the field of adult learning instructional design (Van Dyk et al. 2001:176). Even if the learning experience requires essentially learner-centred strategies, a person still has to be in attendance to facilitate learning (ibid. p. 249).

Facilities

The facilities available for training and producing and presenting the instructional and other material are often constraints considered at the beginning of designing a new programme. It may be necessary to utilise external sources for this purpose. Tracy (1984:247) states that each instructional strategy requires the use of specific types of facilities, media and materials.

Funds

Costs often play a crucial role in many training situations (Van Dyk et al., 2001:249). It is self-evident that the design of a new learning programme will require a considerable amount of funds for the procurements of learning material, the development and production of instructional materials, the possible utilisation of guest speakers during contact sessions and printing costs (SANDF COLET, 2004:6-12).

Procedure for the selection of the delivery method. Table 6 gives a factor and conclusion analysis with regard to the selection of delivery method based on figures 8, 9, 10, 11 and other considerations.

Table 6: Selection of delivery method

Serial No	Factor	Conclusion
1	Nature of the outcomes: High in the cognitive domain. Low in the affective domain.	• In the cognitive and affective domain, it is possible to use any delivery method. • In the psychomotor domain delivery, methods include work groups, intact work group and individualised methods.
2	The target group: The level of adulthood is high and learners have previous experience of democratic delivery methods	Possible delivery methods include: • Group discussion. • Role-play. • Case study. • Individualised (e learning). • Distance education.
3	Content: Learner intellect is from average to high	Learner-Centred methods such as: • Self-study • Individualised (e-learning) • Distance education Group-centred methods such as: • Small group • Intact Work Group • Group discussion • Brain storming • Case study
4	Time: Learners will be available on a part time basis.	• Decentralised approach with contact sessions.
5	Shortlist of Methods	• Correspondence Instruction (Distance education) • Individualised (e-learning) • Small group • Intact work group • Case study
6	Final choice	Distance education (correspondence instruction) with regular contact sessions and elements of small work group and individualised training.

Source: Own

152

Summary

The overall educational approach of distance education is co-operative teaching. This concept could be applied in training for soldiers in the SANDF.

The nature of the programme lies in the need to instruct through various distance education delivery modes, i.e. correspondence courses, contact sessions and digital education (Langholtz et al., 2003:6).

Correspondence instruction (distance education) programmes are planned based on separation of the learning facilitator and the learners. There is often a wide geographical distance between them. Learning facilitators therefore will not have face-to-face contact with learners on a daily basis (Newby et al. 2000:210-214).

The learner has the advantage of working at his/her own pace to acquire knowledge and skills. It involves reading text, undertaking learning activities and sometimes conducting research. The learning material is distributed through the mail or electronically or by means of contact session (Jerling, 1999:150).

This does not mean that there is no guidance and support to the learner. The need for communication in order to ensure that the learner is on the right track in achieving the expected learning outcomes remains. Regular contact sessions will be held to assess learners in their progress towards programme outcomes. As the learning facilitator and the learner both share responsibility for learning there is a need to follow a participatory and adult learning approach (SANDF COLET, 2004: 6) and (De Beer and Mostert, 2005:5).

Correspondence instruction will base on co-operative education involving small heterogeneous groups of learners working together to learn collaboratively while working towards a common academic goal (Newby et al., 2000:92). In this method, learners apply communication and critical-thinking skills to solve problems or to engage in meaningful work together. Students learn from each other when they work on projects as a team (Slavin, 1990: 52-54).

It is a teaching and learning strategy that integrates the learner's academic studies with experiential learning. This is done in partnership with the relevant occupational field based on a mixture of explicit (conceptual and factual) knowledge and tacit knowledge gained through experience and simulation, and by going through the actual process that has to be learned (UNISA, 2003:4). Experiential learning may be facilitated by means of practical projects and/or portfolios aimed at guiding the learner to apply the academic knowledge in a practical or simulated work situation (Langholtz et al, 2003:10).

Furthermore, an outcomes-based approach is followed that underpinning the systems approach to training. Each component of the programme is designated, monitored, and adjusted to the level and pace of instruction as needed. Each learning outcome is established up front and each learner can turn on or off instruction as needed to achieve the desired outcome (Blank, 1982:6).

De Munnik (1997:90) asks the question whether the concepts – outcomes-, standards-, and performance-based education are so different from what institutions have been doing in adult education. The main difference is a shift in emphasis on how the results of the activity are processed.

4.6.3   Learning Aids

Learning aids form part of the communication from the facilitator to the learner and enhances the learning process. Learning aids are the physical learning aids or source of objects, which assist the facilitator in conveying a message or transferring learning (Newby et al., 2000:100).

Learning aids combines material (text, graphics, illustrations, photographs, and facilitation guides) and media (sound, video, and animation). Materials contain messages, while media transmit messages (Jerling, 1999:99). If chosen, and used correctly, all can contribute to learning (Gilley and England, 1989:223).

There are four factors to consider when selecting learning aids, namely; nature of the outcomes, learning content, level of the target group and limitations (Van Dyk et al, 2001:265).

Nature of outcomes and learning content

Learning aids must be selected to meet and suit the outcomes and the learning content. The outcomes and learning content of this programme consist out of a combination of cognitive, psychomotor, and affective skills (ibid, p.265). Distance education programmes are not designed for hands-on skills, or for field exercises. It is recognised that certain psychomotor skills can only be taught under close, direct supervision (Langholtz et al., 2003:7). Therefore, learning aids that can be used successfully in all the domains of learning will receive preference.

<u>Level of target group and learning styles</u>

The content of the learning aids selected were in accordance with the maturity level of the group. Therefore, different learning styles and learning modalities were considered. According to Buckley and Caple (1992:166) knowledge of the learning styles of the target group assist to design programmes that fit in with the main and subordinate styles of learners.

The following learning styles namely: activist, pragmatist, reflector and theorist were complied by Honey and Mumford (1986: 25-29).

Table 7: Learning Styles

Learning Style	Example of learning aid that can be used
Activists Activists enjoy the here and now, dominated by immediate experience and tend to thrive on a short-term crisis. They also tend to thrive on the challenge of new experiences. Activists become bored if they have to implement their ideas. The following are questions that they might ask:	Personal learning aids Multimedia package
• Shall I learn something new? • Will there be a wide variety of different activities? • Will it be appropriate to have fun, have a go, make mistakes or try things out? • Shall I encounter some tough problems or challenges?	
Learning Style	Example of learning aid that can be used
Pragmatists Pragmatists are very practical people. They take the first opportunity to experiment with applications. These people will return from a management course, brimming with new ideas that they want to try out in practice. They respond to problems and opportunities as a "challenge". The following are question that they might ask:	Models Slideshows Multimedia package
• Will there be opportunities to practice and experiment? • Will there be a lot of practical tips and techniques? • Shall we be addressing real problems, will	

it result in action plans to address some of my current problems? • Shall we meet experts who know "how to" and can do it themselves?	

Learning Style	Example of learning aid that can be used
Reflectors Reflectors prefer to stand back and ponder on experiences and observe it from different perspectives. They collect data and analyse it before coming to any conclusion. They consider all possible angles and implications before making a move so they tend to be cautious. They actually enjoy observing other people and often take a back seat at meetings. Reflectors might ask the following questions:	Display Surface Multimedia package Video Computer presentation
• Shall I be given enough time to prepare and consider? • Will there be opportunities and facilities to assemble relevant information? • Will there be opportunities to listen to a variety of points of view? • Shall I be under pressure to improvise or make things up to quickly?	

Learning Style	Example of learning aid that can be used
Theorists Theorists are keen on basic assumptions, principles, theories, models and systems thinking. They value rationality and logic. They tend to be analytical and are unhappy with subjective and ambiguous experiences. They like to make things tidy and fit them into rational schemes: They might ask the following questions:	Transparencies Printed material Multimedia package Computer presentations
• Will there be lots of opportunities to question? • Do the outcomes and programme indicate a clear purpose and structure? • Shall I encounter complex ideas and concepts that will stimulate thinking? • Are the approaches used and the concepts explored sound and valid? • Shall I be with people similar to myself?	

Source: Honey and Mumford, 1986:25

The target group analysis indicated that respondents profiled for this programme are pragmatist - 43%, activist - 23.3% and theorist - 21.1%. Therefore, the learning programme needs to cater for all learning styles especially during contact sessions. It seems that a multimedia media package should satisfy the dominant learning styles. Learning aids will be selected accordingly.

In Kolb's view, sited in a Buckley and Caple (1992:164) acquiring new knowledge, skills and attitudes is a process of confrontation among four modes of experiential learning namely, concrete experience (CE) which involves feeling, reflective observation (RO) involves watching and listening, abstract conceptualisation (AC) involves thinking, and active experimentation (AE) involving doing, making up a cyclic process of learning. To understand leaning modalities two other concepts are important. The first is that each of us is equipped with five senses, namely: sight, hearing, touch, taste and smell. These are the only tools we can use to observe the world around us. There is no other way to know what is happening around us. The second concept expands on the fact that we can only observe the world around us through our senses (SANDF COLET, 2004:16). Although this is the same for all, research has found that there preferences to which senses or combinations of senses are dominant in different individuals. The concept "modality" refers to the route that information takes from the outside world into our human brain. The three modalities are visual, auditory and kinaesthetic (ibid, p.16). A visual learner has visual modality dominance and tends to depend more on sight and less on the other senses. This does not mean that the other senses are ignored, but that they may play a smaller role form time to time. Visual learners focus their sight on the facilitator or what he is doing. They tend to follow the facilitator with their eyes all the time.

They use phrases such as "I see what you mean". Auditory learners depend more on hearing than their other senses. Remember, however, that this does not negate the other senses. They tend to look from side to side during a presentation. This is because they turn to look towards any sound that they hear. Therefore, it is important to keep a check on disruptive noises in and around the learning environment. They also tend to use phrases such as "I hear you" or "this sounds right to me" and they are generally good mimics or storytellers. Kinaesthetic learners favour the sense of touch, while also user their other senses to a lesser extent. How they feel about a subject plays a large role in their learning. They will tend to look down during a presentation as they try to their feelings. They also prefer to sit close together in groups and they like to touch someone as a way of expression. They don't have a very large personal space and they are uncomfortable with individual methods of learning such as study or certain phases of distance learning. They will use phrases like "this feels right to me" or "are you in touch with the group?" (ibid, p.17). The learning modalities of all learners need to be considered when preparing for a learning event. Try to accommodate all learners when determining suitable learning activities and selecting learning aids.

Selection matrix for learning aids. A learning aids selection matrix can help to choose between the various learning aids.

Table 8: Selection matrix for learning aids

Do you have...?	Personal Learning Aids	Transparencies	Printed Material	Display Surfaces *	Models	Multi-media Package	Computer Presentation	Video	Slide Show
1. Adequate development time?		√	√	√	X	√	√	x	x
2. Adequate budget for producing this learning aid?		√	√	√	X	√	√	X	X
3. Adequate facilities to develop this learning aid?		√	√	X	X	√	√	X	X
4. An appropriate learning environment?		X	√	X	X	√	X	√	X
5. The right equipment for this learning aid?	Not for assessment purposes	√	√	X	X	√	√	X	X
6. Opportunities for repeated use?		√	√	X	X	√	√	√	√
7. Which is the right learning aid/s for my organisation's culture?		X	√	X	√	√	√	√	√
		Y N	Y N	Y N	Y N	Y N	Y N	Y N	Y N
8. Can this learning aid be updated easily?		√ √		X	X	X √		X	X
9. Is it a cognitive, affective or psychomotor learning event?		C A	C A	C A	C A	C A	C A	C A	C A
		P	P	P	P	P	P	P	P
(keep in mind the selected domain of the outcome)		Y N	Y N	Y N	Y N	Y N	Y N	Y N	Y N
10. Is this learning aid applicable to the target group?		X √	√	√		X √	√	√	X
(Where Y = Yes or N = No, the Yes will equal a positive mark)									
Total		5	7	3	1	8	6	4	2

1 choice	2nd choice	3 rd choice
Multi-media Package	Printed material	Computer presentation

Source: SANDF COLET, 2004:17

Motivation for the choice of a multi-media Package with printed material and computer presentations as the primary the primary learning aid includes the following: Multi-media packages can be used successfully in cognitive, psychomotor, and affective outcomes. The facilitator can combine a lot of learning aids. Using printed or computer based readers learners are free to stop at any point, and refer. The material can be very portable which enables the learner to study where and when they want. Learning material can be designed in such a way that it allows self-paced instruction. Thus learners can proceed at own pace. Computer presentations will be very useful during contact sessions; Computer presentations can be updated easily when information changes. Computer presentations can be made available to all learners via the internet or compact disc; computer presentations can be used repeatedly and it is not necessary to reproduce them. Facilitation by means of computer is consistent regardless of the facilitator, location or time. Disadvantages include: a multi-media package could be very expensive to develop; it takes a lot of time to set up. Learners must have access to a computer and the internet. (SANDF COLET, 2004:18)

Suggested Multi-media Package.

The following is a proposed package for use during PSO education.

- Learners will receive following:

    - Outcomes.
    - Learning content in the form of printed material and computer discs.
    - Learner workbook containing tests related to each objective.
    - Example of a portfolio of learning (POL).
    - End-of-course examination (provided with learning programme 1).

- Answer Sheet for end-of-course examination (summative).
- Return envelope for end-of-course examination.
- Internet support (e-learning).

- <u>Facilitators notes</u>. These notes deal with the content in the learning package and give guidance to the facilitator concerning the achievement of the outcomes. These notes will refer to available learning aids.

4.6.4   <u>Activities</u>

Activities selected to accompany the learning must enable the learners to meet the outcome of a lesson and must hold the learners interest. It may be necessary to achieve more than one activity for each major lesson, depending on the learning outcome.   However, during distance education the learner and the facilitator is separated and activities will be reserved for contact sessions. In this, section a basic idea of activities that could be used to enable the meet the learning outcomes is formulated. These activities will be planned in more detail during the development of programme material (SANDF COLET, 2004:20). Table 9 gives a scheme of activities that could possible be used during these programmes.

Table 9: Informal learner activities in outcomes-based assessment

Example	Description	Advantage
Group projects	A number of learners work on a task together. This might include discussion and group presentation.	You can assess learners' abilities to work as a team and to complete the task competently.
Oral presentation	Learners present work orally to the learning facilitator/group.	Allows learners' abilities to tell us what they know. Assess both the work completed and the ability to communicate what is learnt.
Written assignment	This could be an essay or other	Allows for the demonstration of learners'

Example	Description	Advantage
	piece of writing that involves discussion and presentation.	thinking (cognitive), writing and communication skills.
Practical assignment	These could be models and posters.	Demonstrates how learners understand certain concepts and how they apply it.
Peer-assessment	Learners give their own opinions of the group's performance, compared to the outcomes they should achieve.	Enhances learner participation.
Portfolio assessment	Files or folders that contain samples of the learners' work done over time.	Allows for the assessment of learners over a period of time. Could be used for recognition of prior learning.
Self assessment	Learners are asked to assess themselves against the given outcomes.	Learners develop an understanding of the learning outcomes.

Source: SANDF COLET, 2004:20

4.6.5   **SUMMARY**

Outcomes-based training programmes are implemented widely.   To ensure success of distance education programmes, a requirement is adult learners who participate actively in the learning process. The training service providers need to provide active guidance and support.   There are various learning theories that must be considered for application to ETD.   It is important to implement learner activities that will encourage "whole brain thinkers".   This section proposed a delivery method, decided on training materials and listed some activities that could be used during programme delivery.   The next section addresses the issue of assessment.

4.7.   **SECTION 6: LEARNER ASSESSMENT**

4.7.1   <u>**INTRODUCTION**</u>

It is of no use when a learning experience has been established for learners but the learning outcomes were not achieved. It is important to assess the entire situation to determine whether the learning was successful, if learning has taken place and if the outcomes have been achieved (SANDF COLET, 2004:121).

4.7.2   <u>**PURPOSE OF ASSESSMENT**</u>

Reid, Barrington and Kennedy (1992:287) add that assessment provides feedback to the facilitator about his/her performance, and indicates the extent to which learning outcomes have been achieved and whether any further training need is to be addressed.

4.7.3   <u>**TYPES OF ASSESSMENT**</u>

The purposes of assessment are reflected in the different types of assessment (Jerling, 1999:220). The following types of learner assessment are considered for this qualification:

Diagnostic assessment is used prior to a learning programme. A pre-test will be taken during the contact session at the beginning of a learning programme. Information gained this way helps the facilitator and assessor to determine the learner's pre-knowledge, pre-skills and pre-attitudes (Newby et al., 2000:222). The completion of this assignment is an entry requirement for the programme, and will be administered on day one of the first contact session (SANDF COLET, 2006b:1).

It will also assist in the process of recognition of prior learning (Van der Spuy, Cronje and Breytenbach, 2005:3) and (Jerling, 1999:220).

Formative assessment takes place during the learning process, serving the following purposes: determine what learners have learned to that point, supply feedback as the learning process occurs, identify what type of additional practice may be needed and refocus learner's attention (Newby et al., 2000:222). Formative assessment thus aims to help learners grow and progress. It is therefore developmental in nature, and allows for feedback, remedial activities as well as additional support (Van der Spuy et al., 2005:3). Assessment will include exercises and self-assessment activities while working through the interactive learning material. All exercises and self assessment activities are completed in writing (end-of-lesson questions in workbook) and this information is placed in the portfolio of evidence.

Feedback is provided on the learner's progress and he/she has the opportunity to improve and to develop. The learner is provided with the opportunity (during contact sessions) to carry out various activities related to the learning material. The purpose is to develop in preparation for final assessment that will take place towards the end during a contact session.

Summative assessment refers to the type of assessment that takes place at the end of a learning programme (Goodwin-Davey, 2004:6). Judgement is made about achievement. It is the final measure of what was learnt (Newby et al., 2000:222). Summative assessments is carried out using written examinations, written assignments, syndicate tasks, role plays and presentations during contact sessions (SANDF COLET, 2003b:122). A learner deem competent or not yet competent because of their assessment against the standard set (Van der Spuy et al., 2005:3).   In OBET, emphasis place on continuous assessment, meaning that assessment is an ongoing process. Simply stated, assessment should take place throughout a period of learning (SANDF COLET, 2004b:14). Outcomes-based assessment is associated with criterion-referenced where assessment is done against the standard that is stated in terms of the specified outcomes and the accompanying laid down assessment criteria (Van der Spuy et al., 2005:3) and (Jerling, 1999:219).

4.7.4   **ASSESSMENT METHODS**

SAQA (2001:27) describe different assessment methods in table 10.

Table 10: Assessment methods

Assessment method	Advantages	Disadvantages
Role-play Assessment of attitudes and interpersonal skills through role-play	An excellent way to get in focus with the affective (feelings) domains of learning. If well managed and structured, it can be satisfying and enjoyable for participants.	Some participants may feel intimidated by having to act out a role-play. A considerable number of sources (such as time for preparation and play) may be required. The evidence obtained might be unpredictable.
Written case study A detailed description of a specific situation that may be genuine or fictional, for example an emergency situation in the workplace that a learner needs to handle according to policies and guidelines.	A good method for providing evidence of a learner's knowledge on procedures, as well as his/her ability to use higher cognitive thinking skills (such as problem-solving and decision-making). A good method to assess all three types of competence (foundational, practical and reflexive).	Learners may react differently in the real-life situation if the case study was fictional. It is time-consuming to design an effective case study. The assessor might not get good evidence if the case study was not properly planned, resulting into a pleasant pastime without any training value.
Written test/examination A selection of written/typed questions, requiring a written response.	Useful to provide evidence on the cognitive domain of learning. The assessment process is standardised. All learners write the same test or examination.	Not suitable for assessing the affective (feelings) and psychomotor (skills) domains of learning. A great amount of time and effort is required to draw up proper questions and a memorandum (model answer)

Assessment method	Advantages	Disadvantages
		for a test or examination.
Group project A project is assigned to a group of learners who work together to achieve the specific outcomes. This might involve oral presentation and discussion.	The learners' abilities to work as a team and to complete the task competently are assessed. It allows for thorough research and investigation. Higher cognitive thinking skills of learners are stimulated (such as critical and creative thinking).	It may be difficult to determine whether it is the learner's own work (authenticity). Not all group members make equal contributions. It is difficult to assess individuals' work.
Written assignment This could be a written assignment that could be an essay or other piece of writing that involves discussion and presentation. It could also be a practical assignment that involves the making of posters and models. It may be assigned to a group of learners or to individuals.	It allows for thorough research and investigation. Higher cognitive thinking skills of learners are stimulated (such as critical and creative thinking). Learners read the material assigned as it appears in the original writing, and do not receive it second-hand.	The assessor must find ways to ensure that the assignment is the learner's own work. The assessor may need more evidence (practical demonstration). Assignment assessment is very time-consuming.
Self assessment A learner assesses his/her own level of competence.	The learner develops a better understanding of the outcomes that have to be achieved. It is a valuable way to find out what a learner thinks about his/her level of performance.	It may not be an accurate form of assessment. Some learners may underestimate their level of competencies while others have unrealistically high opinions of their abilities.
Peer assessment Learners give their own opinions of the groups' performance, compared to the outcomes they should achieve.	Learner participation is enhanced. It confirms competence applied in the work environment. Useful for group work to assess competencies such as "working in a team."	It may not be a true reflection of the learner's competence due to factors such as favouritism or prejudice. The learner might feel threatened by the situation.
Portfolio of evidence (A file or folder that	It allows for the assessment of a learner over a period. It could be use for recognition of prior	It may not be an accurate form of assessment. The assessor must find ways to

Assessment method	Advantages	Disadvantages
contains samples of the learner's work done over time.	learning.	ensure that the assignment is the learner's own work. The assessor may need more evidence (practical demonstration) and clarification.

Source: AWL 2001:6-14

4.7.5   **MANAGEMENT OF ASSESSMENT**

Part of the ETD quality assurance, is the management of evaluation and assessment.   One of the elements in the process is the management of assessment which involves (Van der Spuy et al., 2005:4):

- The preparatory phase for planning and designing of the assessment.
- The learner assessment process:
    - Demonstrate understanding of outcomes-based assessment;
    - Prepare for assessments;
    - Conduct assessments;
    - Provide feedback on assessment, and
    - Review assessments.
- Re-assessment procedure.
- Appeal procedure.
- Moderation process.
- Recognition of Prior Learning (RPL) process.
- Withdrawal and suspension process.

Re-assessment

Rules regarding re-assessment are stated in the curriculum and make provision for the following (Van der Spuy et al., 2005:5):

- The minimum competent level or grading that permits the learner to be re-assessed. The actions to be taken when a learner does not achieve the prescribed minimum competence level/grading during a re-assessment.
- The learner, who fails to be present for the scheduled assessment without a valid reason, forfeits this re-assessment opportunity, which implies a not competent result. The validity shall be determined by a moderating committee.
- Re-assessment should take place in the same situation or context and under the same conditions as the initial assessment. The same method and assessment instrument may be used, but the task and the material should be changed. However, re-assessment should be of the same complexity and level as the previous assessments.
- The learning programme, in which the learner has done a re-assessment, is to be indicated as a re-assessment on all official documents (individual and course reports).
- Only one re-assessment per unsuccessful assessment is permitted.

Supplementary/Special assessment

A learner must be allowed to do a supplementary assessment when he or she was unable to undertake a scheduled summative assessment. This assessment is only valid in the following circumstances: personal Illness and serious Illness or death of a close family member. Before being granted a supplementary assessment, the validity of the circumstances must be investigated and authorised. The supplementary assessment date will be set by the ETDP or registered assessor for this specific assessment. Should a learner be unsuccessful during this supplementary assessment he/she shall be entitled to a re-assessment (Van der Spuy et al., 2005:5).

Repetition of a learning program

The career manager and governing body shall decide if and when a learner may repeat a learning program after a learner has been found guilty of dishonesty by a court of law. If a learner is repeatedly unsuccessful in his/her attempts to demonstrate competence, and the provider has given the learner the necessary support, the learner shall no longer have the opportunity to attend the specific learning program. The maximum opportunities for repeating a learning program are stated in the curriculum. The Provider must submit a request to the governing body with the view to get authorization for the exclusion of the learner from further enrolment of the learning program. The provider shall notify the learner's service or division of the circumstances and recommend alternative ETD or career path for the particular learner (Van der Spuy et al., 2005:5).

4.7.5.4   Appeal Procedure

An appeal procedure ensures that learners may appeal against an assessment decision. The appeal must be towards the assessor who did the assessment, and if unsatisfied, to the internal moderator followed by the external moderator, and in the final instance, to the ETQA. Every Provider shall comply with the prescribed internal DOD ETD appeal procedure, up to the stage where the appeal must be forwarded to the external moderator. For further appeals the

Providers must comply with the appeal procedure of the specific ETQA they are accredited with. Providers and learners shall attempt to resolve matters internally before seeking recourse with the relevant ETQA. A Governing Body/s (board structure) will act as the controlling body for ETD related matters of the providers, within the framework of SAQA regulations prescripts (Van der Spuy et al., 2005:6).

Moderation

Internal moderation of assessment occurs at the Providers and external moderation is the responsibility of the ETQAs. Providers must ensure that specific individuals, who are experienced assessors, manage the internal moderation process. The minimum requirement that internal moderators must comply with is the SAQA ID 115759 "conduct moderation of outcomes-based assessment" or an ETD qualification registered on the NQF, which includes this unit standard. This implies that the individual must have completed the: "conduct outcomes-based assessment" and the "design and develop outcomes-based assessment" unit standard. Moderators must register with the appropriate ETQA of the specific field in which the individual will be moderating (Van der Spuy et al., 2005:6).

Recognition of Prior Learning (RPL)

RPL is defined in the SAQA Act in terms National Standards Bodies (NSB) (Government Gazette, No 18787 of 28 March 1998),: RPL means the comparison of the previous learning and experience of a learner obtained against the learning outcomes required for a specific qualification, and the acceptance for purposes of qualification of that which meets the requirements. The principle of

RPL is broadly stated as the giving of credit to what learners already know and can do, regardless of whether this learning was achieved formally or informally. The process of recognition of prior achievements is about: Identifying what the learner knows and can do and matching the learner's skill, knowledge and experience to specific unit standards and the associated criteria, assessing the learner against the standards, crediting the learner for skills, knowledge and experience built up through formal/informal/non-formal learning that occurred in the past.

There is no fundamental difference in the assessment of previously acquired skills and knowledge and the assessment in current learning program. The learner seeking credits still has to comply with all the requirements stated in the unit standard. The only difference is that the learner will not need to go through a formal learning program. Awarding a credential is not dependent on the time spent in a learning program, but on the learner's readiness to demonstrate competence. A learner that feels ready can present him/herself for assessment and/or submit the necessary evidence as required by the learning outcomes and the assessment criteria, as stated in the registered unit standard. It is furthermore the learner's responsibility to provide evidence of competence in accordance with the relevant outcomes. Although RPL is a "special assessment" it must be incorporated in the existing assessment processes (Van der Spuy et al., 2005:6-7) and (Jerling, 1999:219).

<u>Withdrawal, Suspension and Exclusion from a Learning Program</u>

A learner can be withdrawn/suspended or excluded from a learning program, for the following reasons (Van der Spuy et al., 2005:8):

<u>Reasons for withdrawal</u>. Learners may be withdrawn from a learning program for the following reasons:

- Humanitarian reasons/Learner's own request.
- Medical reasons.
- Operational requirements.
- Insufficient attendance on learning program (residential)

<u>Reasons for suspension/exclusion</u>. Learners may be suspended or excluded from a learning program for the following reasons:

- Below standard achievement/not reaching set outcomes. The following has reference: If a learner is repeatedly unsuccessful in his/her attempts to demonstrate competence, and the provider has given the learner the necessary support, the learner may be suspended from the specific learning program. The fact that a learner did not succeed is not negotiable. The learner may be suspended/excluded from further enrolment, for a specific period determined by the governing body.
- Unacceptable or dishonest behaviour include but is not limited to, the following conduct:

  - Copying the assignments of previous learners and copied answers from another learner during an assessment:

- Possessing and/or use of unauthorised reference material of any nature whatsoever, during an assessment:

- Communicating with other learner(s) during an individualised assessment.

- Assisting a fellow learner during an assessment by providing him/her with answers to the assessment questions, in any manner whatsoever.

- Acting in contravention of instructions regarding the completion of individual tasks, in circumstances where such contravention amounts to dishonesty, as determined by the ETDP, assessment rules, for example.

- Unacceptable or improper behaviour or misconduct includes but is not limited to the following conduct:

  - Absences without official leave (AWOL).

  - Under the influence of alcohol or narcotic drugs.

  - Aggressive behaviour, intimidation, assault or damage to property.

  - Use of foul language or insubordination.

  - Scandalous behaviour or conduct unbecoming DOD personnel.

4.7.6   **CONCLUSION**

Assessment should be conducted in accordance with an assessment plan. It is a participatory approach and the assessor is there to help the learner to produce evidence that proves that he/she is competent. Proper records should be kept. This forms part of quality assurance. Feedback should be provided to the learner regarding his/her competence level. The learner has the right to be re-assessed or to appeal against the assessment result.

4.8 SECTION 7: PROGRAMME EVALUATION

4.8.1 INTRODUCTION

According to Sheal (1994:183), assessment has three main purposes namely, to improve ETD programmes, to assess the value of ETD to the learners and to assess the value of ETD to the organisation. These three purposes of evaluation are reflected in the different types of evaluation; formative and summative, and different levels of evaluation; reaction, behaviour, learning and results (Jerling, 1999:220). According to Rothwell and Stredi (1992:144) evaluation is a process of appraising something carefully to determine its value. It involves judging the worth of planned learning experiences. Goldstein (quoted in Bramley, 1991:87) defines evaluation as the systematic collection of descriptive and judgemental information necessary to make effective decisions related to the selection, adoption, value and modification of various instructional activities. The purpose of this section is to give an indication of how programme evaluation will be done.

4.8.2 FORMATIVE EVALUATION

Formative evaluation involves continuous evaluation during the development of ETD (Sheal, 1994:184). The purpose of this type of evaluation is to improve the quality of ETD programmes (Jerling, 1999:219). Formative evaluation is concerned with decisions taken while the ETD design is being developed and the learning materials being produced (Van Dyk et al., 1992:213). The formative evaluation of the design report and curriculum will entail a reputability study. This involves the evaluation of the research promoter Dr K. de Beer and second promoter (external) Prof Harvey Langholtz. Each expert will receive a draft copy of the design report, which includes the contents of the proposed curriculum. After the experts have had an opportunity to review and assess the material, the researcher will correct shortfalls and present then with a final copy. The experts voice their opinion on the learning program contents and the method of implementation (Bless & Higson-Smith, 1995:50). These comments and criticisms form the base of the formative evaluation.

8.3 SUMMATIVE EVALUATION

Summative evaluation takes place after ETD programme has been completed (Jerling, 1999:220). Perhaps the best-known methodology is Kirkpatrick's four level evaluation models of reaction, learning, performance, and impact (Clark, 2000). The figure below shows how the evaluation process fits together.

Figure 12: Levels of Training Evaluation

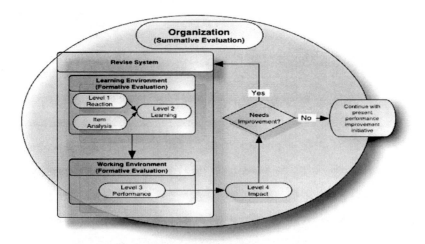

Source: Clark (2000) - http://www.nwlink.com.

Level One - Reaction

Evaluating reaction can be seen as the same as measuring customer satisfaction. If ETD is to be effective, it is important that learners react favourably to it. Otherwise they will not be motivated to learn. They will also tell others of their reactions, and this could influence decisions to reduce or eliminate the programme (Kirkpatrick, 1994:27). This level is often measured with attitude questionnaires that are passed out after most training classes. This level measures one thing: the learner's perception (reaction) of the learning program. Learners are keenly aware of what they need to know to accomplish a task. If the training program fails to satisfy their needs, a determination should be made as to whether it's the fault of the program design or delivery. This level is not indicative of the training's performance potential as it does not measure what new skills the learners have acquired or what they have learned that will transfer back to the working environment. This has caused some evaluators to down play its value. However, the interest, attention and motivation of the participants are critical to the success of any training program. People learn better, when they react positively to the learning environment. When the learning package is first presented, the learner has to make a decision as to whether he or she will pay attention to it. If the goal or task is judged as important and achievable, then the learner is normally motivated to engage in it (Markus and Ruvulo, 1990:211-241).

Level Two - Learning

It is important to measure learning because no change in behaviour (level three) can take place if learning has not occurred (Kirkpatrick, 1994:43). This is the extent to which participants change attitudes, improve knowledge, and increase skill as a result of attending the program. It addresses the question: did the participants learn anything? The learning evaluations require post-testing to ascertain what skills were learned during the training. In addition, the post-testing is only valid when combined with pre-testing, to differentiate between what learners already knew prior to training and what they actually learned during the learning program. Measuring the learning that takes place in a training program is important in order to validate the learning objectives. Evaluating the learning that has taken place typically focuses on such questions as: What knowledge was acquired? What skills were developed or enhanced? What attitudes were changed? Learner assessments are created to allow a judgment to be made about the learner's capability for performance. There are two parts to this process: the gathering of information or evidence (testing the learner) and the judging of the information (what does the data represent?). This assessment should not be confused with evaluation. Assessment is about the progress and achievements of the individual learners, while evaluation is about the learning program as a whole (Tovey, 1997:88).

Evaluation in this process comes through the learner assessment that was built in the design phase. The assessment instrument normally has more benefits to the designer than to the learner because for the designer, the building of the assessment helps to define what the learning must produce. For the learner, assessments are statistical instruments that normally poorly correlate with the realities of performance on the job and they rate learners low on the "assumed" correlatives of the job requirements. Thus, the next level is the preferred method of assuring that the learning transfers to the job, but sadly, it is quite rarely performed (Gilbert, 1998:93).

Level Three - Performance (behaviour)

In Kirkpatrick's original four-levels of evaluation, he names this level "behaviour." However, behaviour is the action that is performed, while the final results of the behaviour are the performance. Gilbert (1998:94) said that performance has two aspects - behaviour being the means and its consequence being the end. If only worried about the behavioural aspect, then this could be done in the training environment. However, the consequence of the behaviour (performance) is what is important after - can the learner now perform in the working environment? This evaluation involves testing the students capabilities to perform learned skills while on the job, rather than in the classroom. Level three evaluations can be performed formally (testing) or informally (observation). It determines if the correct performance is now occurring by answering the question, "Do people use their newly acquired learning's on the job?" It is important to measure performance because the primary purpose of training is to improve results by having the students learn new skills and knowledge and then actually applying them to the job. Learning new skills and knowledge is no good to an organization unless the participants actually use them in their work activities. Since level three measurements must take place after the learners have returned to their jobs, the actual level three measurements will typically involve someone closely involved with the learner, such as a supervisor. Although it takes, a greater effort to collect this data than it does to collect data during training, its value is important to the training department, organization as the data provides insight into the transfer of learning from the classroom to the work environment, and the barriers encountered when attempting to implement the new techniques learned in the program.

Level Four - Results

These results measure the training program's effectiveness, that is, "what impact has the training achieved?" These impacts can include such items as monetary, efficiency, moral, and teamwork. While it is often difficult to isolate the results of a training program, it is usually possible to link training contributions to organizational improvements. Collecting, organizing and analyzing level four information can be difficult, time-consuming and more costly than the other three levels, but the results are often quite worthwhile when viewed in the full context of its value to the organization. Moving from level one to level four, the evaluation process becomes more difficult and time-consuming; however, it provides information that is of increasingly significant value. Perhaps the most frequently type of measurement is level one because it is the easiest to measure. However, it provides the least valuable data. Measuring results that affect the organization is considerably more difficult, thus it is conducted less frequently, yet it yields the most valuable information. Each evaluation level should be used to provide a cross set of data for measuring training program. The first three-levels of Kirkpatrick's evaluation - reaction, learning, and performance are largely "soft" measurements, however decision-makers who approve such training programs, prefer results (returns or affects). That does not mean the first three are useless, indeed, their use is in tracking problems within the learning package:

- Reaction informs how relevant the training is to the work the learners perform (it measures how well the training requirement analysis processes worked).
- Learning informs to the degree of relevance that the training package worked to transfer KSAs from the training material to the learners (it measures how well the design and development processes worked).

- The performance level informs of the degree that the learning can actually be applied to the learner's job (it measures how well the performance analysis process worked).

- Impact informs of the "return" the organization receives from the training. Decision-makers prefer this harder "result," although not necessarily in dollars and cents. A recent study of financial and information technology executives found that they consider both hard and soft "returns" when it comes to customer-centric technologies, but give more weight to non-financial metrics (soft), such as customer satisfaction and loyalty, for example (Hayes, 2003:18).

Note the difference in "information" and "returns." That is, the first three-levels give "information" for improving the learning package. While the fourth-level gives "impacts." A hard result is generally given in rand and cents, while soft results are more informational in nature, but instead of evaluating how well the training worked, it evaluates the impact that training has upon the organization. In this case, however, there is an exception, as the target organisational vision is to provide learning opportunities. This final measurement of the learning program might be met with a more balanced approach or a "balanced scorecard" (Kaplan and Norton, 2001 in Clark, 2000), which looks at the impact or return from four perspectives:

- Financial: A measurement, such as a Return on Investment (ROI), that shows a monetary return, or the impact itself, such as how the output is affected. Financial can be either soft or hard results.

- Customer: Improving an area in which the organization differentiates itself from competitors to attract, retain, and deepen relationships with its targeted customers.

- Internal: Achieve excellence by improving such processes as supply-chain management, production process, or support process.

- Innovation and Learning: Ensuring the learning package supports a climate for organizational change, innovation, and the growth of individuals.

4.8.4   **SUMMARY**

In this section the evaluation of the proposed learning program was discussed. Two types of evaluation can be distinguished, namely formative and summative evaluation. Formative evaluation involves a continuous process in which the programme is evaluated while it is being developed. A reputability study will be carried out to finalise the formative evaluation. Summative evaluation is done after the ETD programme has been conducted, and its purpose is to evaluate the effectiveness of the programme. A detail assessment plan has yet to be developed. Four levels of summative evaluation can be distinguished, namely reaction, learning, performance and results. Assessment should not be confused with evaluation. Assessment is about the progress and achievements of the individual learners, while evaluation is about the learning program as a whole

4.9   **CONLUSION**

This chapter is an account of the results of the study according to the research objectives stated. The survey results indicate that there is training gap, and confirm that there is a need amongst SA Army officers in the SANDF to participate in a tertiary program on PSO in Africa. It also answers the question on the best method to design such learning program. Section 2 presented a job description and target group analysis. Section 3 aligned the generic job requirement of a peacekeeper with the training needs. Sections 4, 5, 6, and 7 described the development of ETD opportunities with reference to the development, delivery and assessment of ETD opportunities. The next chapter reflects findings and recommendations concerning a programme strategy and possible curriculum content.

CHAPTER 5 - FINDINGS AND RECOMMENDATIONS

5.1   **INTRODUCTION**

The purpose of this chapter is to present a summary of the findings, conclusions and recommendations with due consideration of the objectives of the study. It consists of the observations and conclusions made from the study, reveals the possible limitations of the study and makes recommendations on a programme strategy and curriculum. The chapter concludes with recommendations regarding further research and larger relevance and value of the study.

5.2   **SUMMARY OF FINDINGS AND CONCLUSIONS**

Findings indicate that there is a problem with regard to training on PSO in Africa. The study also concludes that there is a need for a Model of Co-operative Education on PSO in Africa.

If the RSA wants to play a leading role on an economic and politically unstable continent, it must have a focussed and functional defence force in order to negotiate from a position of strength.

The near future continues to hold a high demographic risk of civil conflict in Africa. South Africa remains a state in transition and will for some time to come. The international community expects South Africa to become more involved in peacekeeping missions. The focus of main effort of the SANDF should therefore be on PSO in Africa.

The SANDF, however, has a limited capacity to deploy troops in PSO over long periods. It has neither the logistical, nor the personnel capacity to do so. The defence budget remains under pressure to such an extent that South African military potency is slipping and will drop further if the lack of political will continues to hamper the effectiveness of the SANDF.

Most important is that the SANDF needs to have a strong civilian-military coordination mindset, as there is prior deployment of other organisations in the conflict region. The focus of the SANDF force from the onset should therefore be one of development in cooperation with other stakeholder organisations.

Unfortunately, the country faces many challenges that have an influence on the productivity and its competitiveness in the global market. This is mainly due to low levels of education and training. Knowledge is power that determines the competitiveness of a country. It is clear that there is a demand for ETD in the SANDF which will most likely increase.

The South African Department of Defence (DOD) has to align the ETD of all its members with international and national trends. The NQF is South Africa's answer to global and national demands for a change in the approach to ETD. There is a huge transformation in the field of ETD, with the NQF forming the centre of gravity.

Training peacekeepers via distance education is an inexpensive means for Institutions of Higher Learning to get involved and contribute. This could be a key step to assist in the development of modern, professional armed forces.

A Model of Co-operative Education on PSO in Africa could provide training and education for military practitioners from the SANDF and SADC countries, diplomats, civilian employees of ministries of defence, foreign affairs, and employees of NGOs, scholars and serious citizens in order to improve their ability to participate in multinational peace support and humanitarian operations.

5.3   **LIMITATIONS**

The results of this research are interpreted with recognition of certain limitations. These limitations link with sources of error mentioned in Chapter 3 of the study. The generalisation of the results is limited to the degree to which other populations resemble the one studied.

It is possible that a sample of soldiers will yield unique results in that warfare is a male dominated profession, has mandatory training and experiences higher turnover rates than many other professions.

The sample was also limited to the units of the SA Army (School of Air Defence Artillery, School of Armour, SA Army College, Army Support Base Kimberley, 10 Anti-aircraft Regiment). In addition, as respondents were full-time soldiers, employed at full time force units, the findings may not apply to soldiers in other settings such as the reserve or part-time forces.

The survey nature of the study introduces limitations that are inherent in the research design, including the possible ambiguity of individual questions, answers that not clarified memory lapses, variation in individual motivation and variations in the knowledge of the respondents. This is noted as being especially relevant for studies of the perceptions of work-related practices.

RECOMMENDATIONS

The consideration, development and adoption of these recommendations will provide the different stakeholders an avenue for the effective participation of Institutions of Higher Learning in the peace drive in Africa by presenting a Model of Co-operative Education on PSO in Africa:

The non-availability of a Model of a Co-operative Education on PSO in Africa within Institutions of Higher Learning makes this a feasible project.

Partnerships for co-operation should be formed with the Central University of Technology, Free State (CUT); the University of South Africa (UNISA); The SA National Defence Force College of Educational Technology (COLET); The Northern Cape Institute for Higher Learning (NIHE), the South African National War College (SANWC) and the Institute for Security Studies (ISS) in order to establish a sound knowledge base on PSO in Africa.

Marketing strategy should be to aggressively enhance, promote and support the fact that the envisaged product will be unique, due to the fact that no Institution of Higher Learning in South Africa currently has a similar programme based on scientific instructional design.

Sales strategy need to consist out of making the product available at a competitive price in order to capture market share before the entrance of other competitors especially from the international arena.

Profit goals could be established later when the Institute of Higher Learning has a consistent sales volume and customer base. Financial projections indicate that the exit of investment will be achievable within one year.

The SANDF could subscribe to the program in order to give its officers a higher learning qualification (tertiary) in an applicable field. The SANDF could subscribe to the program in order equip its members with non-combat skills that includes a wide variety of PSO subjects. The learning program would be of great assistance to educate the SA community and humanitarian aid organisations with non-combat skills on PSO. The Institute of Security Studies (ISS) could become an important role player in the compilation of instructional content focussed on the African continent.

The ISS could form a partnership with the other mentioned role players to further, and enhance a culture of peace in the South African community. Offering the program to other African countries in line with NEPAD initiatives could enhance capacity building.

The programme strategy provides an overview of the learning programme, its components and the context within which it is presented. It acts as a guide to the ETD practitioner and the learner on the learning programme, standards and expectations. The programme strategy document forms part of the evidence of learning programme alignment to the Outcomes Based format.

The benefits of a programme strategy are that it provides details of the strategy and approach to be used for the learning programmes, informs readers about the purpose and intent of the learning programme, is a record for audit purposes, is used as a discussion document to establish agreement between the designer and the stakeholders on what the programme must achieve and broadly how it is going to be achieved and serves as the basis for developing learning programmes in that it directs efforts.

5.5   FURTHER RESEARCH

Further research must explore the full development of the proposed Model of Co-operative Education on PSO in Africa.   It must also investigate the possibility of applying the model to the rest of Africa.   Ideally, such a study would involve larger samples and include all the Services of a defence force.   It is with such effort that higher education can develop into a major role player in the continued search for peace on the African continent.

5.6   LARGER RELEVANCE AND VALUE OF THE STUDY

There are various international programmes on peacekeeping operations. At present there is, however, no higher learning programme on generic PSO presented by any of the major universities in South Africa.

Our principal product will consist of a Co-operative Education programme on PSO in Africa presented by means of correspondence instruction (distance education) and e-learning.   Product technology will consist of scientific instructional design and development. In response to demonstrated needs in the market, a new learning programme will be developed that includes a feasibility study, a comprehensive instructional design report, the development of quality learning material and the evaluation of the entire programme on PSO in Africa.

This new programme is especially useful to military practitioners, diplomats, civilian employees of ministries of defence, foreign affairs, employees of NGOs, scholars and serious citizens who can now easily benefit from tertiary education.

The key factors in production of the learning programme include scientific instructional design, collaboration and the forming of partnerships with institutions such as the SANDF, the UN Institute for Training and Research Programme on Peacekeeping Operations Correspondence Instruction (UNITAR POCI), UNISA (University of South Africa), the Institute for Security Studies (ISS), SA National War College (SANWC) and the SANDF College of Educational Technology (SANDF COLET).

Delivery includes a comprehensive design report and a curriculum. A complete set of learning material on PSO ready for correspondence instruction will be developed, should the proposed programme be selected for implementation.

As stated, the market for ETD in the field of PSO is growing rapidly, as South Africa is becoming increasingly involved in peacekeeping missions on the African continent. The target market of potential learners includes military practitioners from the SANDF and SADC countries, diplomats, civilian employees of ministries of defence, foreign affairs, employees of NGOs, scholars and serious citizens who could benefit from a learning programme in PSO. The typical customer of this product is someone who is working in the PSO and humanitarian relief related fields and currently deployed or envisaged to be deployed on peacekeeping missions in Africa.

Organisations that could compete in this market are all institutions of higher learning within South Africa. As stated, currently there is no institution of higher learning in the RSA that presents a programme on PSO. UNISA has indicated that it has an interest in presenting courses from UNITAR POCI, but to date nothing has materialised.

Key factors that have resulted in the present competitive position include the non-availability of a higher learning programme on PSO within Institutions of Higher Learning, the willingness of Prof H. Langholtz, the director of the UNITAR POCI in New York to play an active role in the project as part of the study leadership team, the possibility of a partnership agreement with UNITAR POCI and the fact that the current Minister of Defence, Mr M. Lekota, is the chancellor of the CUT. This could result in an early partnership agreement with the SANDF, i.e. before the project is completed.

Current training programmes of the SANDF or other defence forces are not regarded as competition, as these courses are mostly on the tactical level and not diploma/degree accredited. The ability to present a locally designed PSO higher learning programme will be a capability unique to the Higher Learning Institute that decides to present the programme.

To manoeuvre into the most advantageous position prior to taking action, follow the science of planning and directing a project. The forging of cooperation relationships with relevant stakeholders will substantiate the fitness for considerable growth and accomplishment in the area of PSO. Academic development, design and curriculating an accredited UN PSO Higher Learning Programme will assist Institutions of Higher Learning to make a positive contribution towards establishing peace in Africa. Collaborating and a possible franchise to customise (Africanise) the UNITAR courses for the SANDF is a reality. Partnerships with other stakeholders such as the UN, SANDF, ISS, SANDF COLET could enhance capacity building in the sphere of peace.

Offering the programme to other African countries in line with NEPAD initiatives, institutes of higher learning could make a significant contribution to research and development in the field of generic PSO in Africa. Accepting the programme the SANDF gets the opportunity to enhance the knowledge, skills and attitudes (KSAs) of it officers to meet the challenges faced in the Africa PSO theatre.

Officers at all levels in the chain of command would receive sufficient and appropriate training concerning non-combat skills essential for PSO. Officers at all levels of the chain of command will be able to provide adequate supervision of the training preparations undertaken for PSO.

5.7   **CONCLUSION**

Finally, the study concludes that the means to resolve the challenge of institutions of higher learning to assist in the peace drive in Africa is through academic selection, experiential training support and lifelong learning commitments to peacekeeping instruction. Within the overall educational philosophy of a combination of correspondence instruction and co-operative raining, the nature of the proposed project is to fulfil the urgent need to change [2]South Africans into unbiased diplomats.

---

[2]"The assumption that time is a determining factor in the acquisition of knowledge and mastery of skills needs to be confronted" (p 25) and "learning programme developers would be wise to take cognisance of the reality that learners learn differently and come to a learning experience with different levels of understanding and build in appropriate assessment processes to assess what students know rather than what they do not know, and avoid making assumptions about their knowledge base. Teaching strategies naturally should also take this into account. In fact, it could be argued that the successful implementation of the NQF requires that these assumptions are made explicit, so that learners and teachers can work together to ensure that the achievement of all learning outcomes deemed necessary." p 26. Spady as referred to in SAQA: *The National Qualifications Framework and Curriculum Development.* May 2000.

List of References

Africa Contemporary Record. 1981. <u>Annual survey and documents</u>. Africana Publishing Company, Volume XII 1979-80, p.C97.

Allen, G. 1998. <u>Supervision</u>. http://ollie.dcc.educ/mgmt1374/book (retrieved. June 4, 2005).

Amersfoort, H., H. Roozenbeek and C. P. M. Klep. 1999. <u>Netherlands peace support</u> <u>operations</u>. Den Haag: Jellema Grafische Groep.

AWL. 2001. <u>Assessment</u>. Modules 1-5.

Badenhorst, J.C.C and K.J. de Beer. 2004. <u>The role of blended learning in supporting</u> <u>learning in higher education</u>. INTERIMI, Interdisciplinary Journal, Year 3 Number 1. Central University Free State.

Baig, K. 2002. <u>Logistical support to United Nations peacekeeping operations</u>. New York: UNITAR POCI.

Bernadin, H.J. and J.E. Russell. 1993. <u>Human resource management: An experiential</u> <u>approach</u>. New York: McGraw-Hill.

Blank, W.E. 1982. <u>Handbook for developing competency-based training programs</u>. Englewood Cliffs: Prentice Hall.

Bless C., and C. Higson-Smith. 1995. <u>Fundamentals of social research methods: an African</u> <u>perspective. Ed 2</u>. Cape Town: Juta & Co.

Boshoff, H. 2004. <u>African peacekeeping force: SA stretched to its limits</u>. Financial Mail, 18 Jun 04, p.25.

Bouvier, A.A. 2000. <u>International humanitarian law and the law of armed conflict</u>. New York: UNITAR POCI.

Boutros-Ghali, B. 1996. <u>In: United Nations. The Blue Helmets: a review of United Nations</u> <u>peacekeeping, 3rd Ed</u>. New York: UN Department of Public Information.

Bramley, P. 1991. <u>Evaluating training effectiveness</u>. Berkshire: McGraw-Hill Book Company.

Briggs, L.J. 1977. <u>Instructional design</u>. New Jersey: Englewood Cliffs.

Brown, F.B. and Y. Brown. 1994. <u>Distance education around the world. In B. Willis (Ed.),</u> <u>Distance education: Strategies and tools (p.3-39)</u>. Englewood Cliffs, NJ: Educational Technology Publications.

Buckley, R. and J. Caple. 1992. The theory and practice of training. Reading Mass.: Addison-Wesley

Buur, L, H. Vienola, L. Ohlsson, and A. Terp. 2002. Norcaps PSO: Tactical Volume 1, Ed 3. Gummerus Kirjapaino Oy Jyvaskyla.

Buur, L, H. Vienola, L. Ohlsson, and A. Terp. 2002. Norcaps PSO: Tactical Volume 2, Ed 3. Gummerus Kirjapaino Oy Jyvaskyla.

Camp, R.R., P.N. Blanchard, and G.E. Huszco. 1986. Towards a more organisationally effective training strategy and practice. Englewood Cliffs, NY: Prentice-Hall.

Canada Department of National Defence. 2000. Peace support operations field book. Canada: Peace Support Training Centre.

Carnevale, A.P., L.J. Gainer, and A.S. Meltzer. 1990. Workplace basics training manual. San Francisco: Jossey-Bass.

Chang, R.Y. 1994. Creating high IMPACT training: a practical guide to successful training outcomes. Irvine, CA: Richard Chang.

Charter of the United Nations. 1945.

Cilliers, J. 1999. An emerging South African foreign policy identity? Pretoria: Institute for Security Studies, Occasional Paper No.93 – April.

Cilliers, J. 2003. Peace and security through good governance: a guide to the NEPAD African peer review mechanism. Pretoria: Institute for Security Studies.

Cilliers, J. 2004. Human security in Africa: a conceptual framework for review. Pretoria: African human security initiative.

Cincotta, R.P., R. Engelman, and D. Anastasion. 2003. The security demographic: population and civil conflict after the cold war. Washington: Population action international.

Clark, D. 2000. Introduction to instructional system design. http://www.nwlink.com.

Collier, P. 2004. Natural resources and conflict in Africa. Crimes of war project: Wars in Africa.

Conoir, Y. 2002. The Conduct of humanitarian relief operations: principles of intervention and management. New York: UNITAR POCI.

Corbett, M and M.K. Le Rog. 2003. Research methods in political science, Ed 5. Canada: Thomson learning.

Daniels, p. 2005. Towards peace and stability in Africa: the role of south africa. Stellenbosch university: centre for military studies (cemis),

De Beer, K.J. and H.J. Langholtz. 2003. <u>Co-operative training of African peacekeepers through correspondence instruction</u>. Bloemfontein: Central University of Technology.

De Beer, K.J. and J.W. Mostert. 2005. <u>Poster: Collaboration for higher education distance education through United Nations structures in Africa</u>. Durban: University KwaZulu-Natal. SAARDHE – conference, 26-29 June.

Deen, T. 2006. <u>UN peacekeepers could reach 140,000</u>. New York: Janes Defence Weekly. Vol 43. Issue 47. Nov 22.

De Munnik, E.O. 1997. <u>Outcomes-based education and training</u>. Pretoria: SANDF bulletin for educational technology, Oct 97.

De Vries, R. 1997. <u>South African Department of Defence: education, training and development in transformation</u>. Pretoria.

De Cenzo, D.A. and S.P. Robbins. 1994. <u>Human resources management concepts and practices</u>. New York: John Wiley and Sons.

Dick, W., and L. Carey.1996. <u>The systematic design of instruction</u>. New York: Harper Collins.

Donoghue. M and A. Wilkinson. 2003. <u>Mine Action: Humanitarian impact, technical aspects, and global initiatives</u>. New York: UNITAR POCI.

Engelbrecht, L. 2002. <u>Towards an indigenous military: peacebuilding initiative for Africa</u>. African Armed Forces 30 June, p. 22

Ernst, E.A. 2000. <u>Skills development: handbook for SETA'S, employers, and employees in South Africa</u>. Pretoria: College for Comptence.

Erasmus, B.J., and P.S. Van Dyk. 1999. <u>Training management in South Africa. Ed 2</u>. Cape Town: Oxford University Press.

Fabricius, P. 2003. <u>Africa looking to enforce the peace</u>. Cape Times, 28 May, p. 11.

Faure, J.M. 1996. <u>Commanding United Nations peacekeeping operations: methods and techniques for peacekeeping on the ground</u>. New York: UNITAR POCI.

Forster. L. 1997. <u>UN civilian police: restoring order following hostilities</u>. New York: UNITAR POCI.

French Ministry of Defence, Presentation of a talk concerning the concept of the use of French troops in PSO, paper presented at the UNIDIR Workshop on differing national perspectives on UN PSO, op. cit.

Galbraith, J.K. 1967. <u>The new instructional state</u>. Boston: Houghton, Mifflin.

Gilley, J.W. and S.A. England. 1989. Principles of human resource development. Reading: Addison-Wesley.

Gilbert, T. 1998. A leisurely look at worthy performance. The 1998 ASTD training and performance yearbook. Woods, J. & Gortada, J. (editors). New York: McGraw-Hill.

Gleichmann. C, M. Odenwald, K. Steenken and A. Wilkinson. 2004. Disarmament, demobilisation and reintegration a practical field and classroom guide. Frankfurt: Druckerei Hassmüller Graphische Betriebe GmbH & Co. KG,

Goodwin-Davey, A. 2004. Quality assessment in distance education: Principles and processes. Pretoria: UNISA, Institute for Curriculum and Learning Development.

Hayes, M. 2003. Just who's talking return on Investment? Information Week. Feb 03, p.18.

Hårleman, C. 2003. An introduction to the UN System: orientation for serving on a UN field mission. New York: UNITAR POCI.

Hårleman, C. 1997. UN military observers: methods and techniques for serving on a UN observer mission. New York: UNITAR POCI.

Harrison, R. 1989. Training and development. London: IPM.

Heinrich, R., M. Molenda, J.D. Russell, and S. Smaldino. 1999. Instructional media and technologies for learning, Ed 4. Upper Saddle River, NJ: Merrill/Prentice-Hall.

Heitman, Helmoed-Römer, 2003. Analysis: rebirth in Africa. Janes Defence Weekly. Vol 40. Issue 2. 16 July 2003.

Heitman, Helmoed-Römer, 2005. Interview, Lieutenant General Solly Shoke, Chief of the South African Army, We see ourselves as a defence partner in Africa. Janes Defence Weekly. Vol 42. Issue 29. 20 July 2005a.

Heitman, Helmoed-Römer, 2005. Africa: security is the key. Janes Defence Weekly. Vol 42. Issue 29. 20 July 2005b.

Herrly, P.F. 2005. The Impact of peacekeeping and stability operations on the armed forces. Heritage Foundation Lecture No. 915.

Higate, P. 2004. Gender and peacekeeping: case studies: the Democratic Republic of the Congo and Sierra Leone. Pretoria: Institute for Security Studies.

Honey, P and A. Mumford. 1986. The manual of learning styles. Maidenhead, Berkshire: Honey.

Huldt, B.O. 1995. Working multilaterally: the old peacekeepers' viewpoint, in Donald C F Daniel and Bradd C Hayes (eds.), Beyond Traditional Peacekeeping, New York: St. Martin's Press, p. 103.

International Quality and Productivity Centre. 2006. Peacekeeping, reconstruction and stability operations in Africa: deploying successful support, peacekeeping and developmental Missions in Africa. Johannesburg: iqpc.co.za (accessed 28 Feb 2006).

James, A. 1990. Peacekeeping in international politics. London: Macmillan and the International Institute for Strategic Studies.

Jankielsohn, R. 2003. SANDF is becoming overstretched, underfunded, DA. Citizen, 15 December. p. 21.

Jerling, K. 1999. Education, training and development in organisations. Cape Town: Kagiso Tertiary.

Katzenellenbogen, J. 2004. SA's peace role 'at its peak'. Business day, 07 April 2004, p.3.

Kent, V and M. Malan. 2003. Decisions, decisions South Africa's foray into regional peace operations. Pretoria: Institute for Security Studies.

Kirkpatrick, D. 1994. Evaluating training programs. San Francisco, CA: Berrett-Koehler Publishers, Inc.

Klasen, S and F. Zulu. nd. Poverty, inequality and security in South Africa. p. 43-62.

Klingebiel, S. 2005. Africa's new peace and security architecture: converging roles of external actors and African interests. African Defence Review Vol 14, No2.

Knirk, F.G. and K.L. Gustafson. 1986. Instructional technology: A systematic approach to education. New York: Holt, Rhinehart, and Winston.

Kruys, G. 2004. Lessons from African wars: implications for the SANDF. Pretoria: Institute for Security Studies University of Pretoria, Strategic Review for Southern Africa, Vol XXVI, No 1.

Langenbach, M. 1993. Curriculum models in adult education. Malabar: Krieger.

Langholtz H.J., K.J. De Beer, and J. Mostert. 2003. Co-operative instruction for African soldiers in peacekeeping operations. New York: United Nations Institute for Training Research.

Langholtz H.J., K.J. De Beer, and J. Mostert. 2005. Co-Operative education for African militia. Abstract for the Co-operative Education Conference Boston USA 2005.

Lategan L. O. K., W. Vermeulen, and M. Truscott. 2003. Research made easy; a general overview of the research process and context. Bloemfontein: Tekskor BK.

Leslie. D. 2004. The provision of troops and contingent-owned equipment and the method for reimbursement. New York: UNITAR POCI.

Leslie. D. 1999. Operational logistical support of UN peacekeeping missions: intermediate logistics. New York: UNITAR POCI.

Liu. F.T. 1999. The history of UN peacekeeping operations during the Cold War: 1945 to 1987. New York: UNITAR POCI.

Liu. F.T. 1998. The History of UN peacekeeping operations following the Cold War: 1988 to 1997. New York: UNITAR POCI.

Lykke. A.F. 1997. Defining military strategy. Military Review January – February 1997.

Malan, M. 1996. Surveying the middle ground: conceptual issues and peacekeeping In Southern Africa. Pretoria: Training for Peace Project, Institute for Defence Policy Occasional Paper No 2 - March 1996, p.11.

Malan, M. 1998. Peacekeeping in the new millennium: towards 'fourth generation' peace operations. African Security Review, Vol 7, No3.

Mandela, N. 1993. South Africa's future foreign policy. Pretoria: Foreign affairs. Vol 72-5. Nov-Dec.

Markus, H. and A. Ruvulo. 1990. Possible selves. personalized representations of goals; goal concepts in psychology. Hillsdale, NJ: Lawrence Erlbaum. Pp. 211-241.

Medhurst. P. 2002. Global terrorism. New York: UNITAR POCI.

Medhurst. P. 2002. Security for UN Peacekeepers. New York: UNITAR POCI.

Ministry of Defence United Kingdom. 2003. Peace support operations. Llangennech: MOD CSE Joint warfare publication 3-50.

Modise, J. 1997. Facing the future, presentation on the South African Army and transformation. Pretoria: ISS papers 21 Apr. p. 2.

Morris, M. 2003. Shouldn't we first solve our own problems? Cape Argus 19 Aug, p.12.

Mouton, J. 2001. How to succeed in your master's & doctoral studies; a South African guide and resource book. Pretoria: Van Schaik.

Nadler, L. 1982. Designing training programmes: The critical events model. Reading, Mass.: Addison-Wesley.

Neethling, T. 1999. Suid Afrika en vredesteunoperasies: perspektiewe op uitgangspunte en oorwegings. Bloemfontein: University of the Free State.

Nel, P.S., P.D. Gerber, P.S. van Dyk, H. Schultz, and T.J. Sono.2001. Human resources management. Cape Town: Oxford University Press.

Newby, T.J., Stepich, D.A., Lehman, J.D, and Russell, J.D. 2000. Instructional technology for teaching and learning, Ed 2. New Jersey: Prentice Hall.

Netherlands Ministry of Defence. 2000. Peace operations, army publication part III. Netherlands.

Olivier, C. 1998. How to educate and train outcomes-based. Pretoria: Van Schaik.

Pan, E. 2005. African peacekeeping operations council on foreign relations. http://www.cfr.org/publication/9333/african_peacekeeping_operations.html.

Papp, D.S. 1988. Contemporary international relations: frameworks for understanding, Ed 2. New York: MacMillan.

Potgieter, J. 1996. Evolution of a national doctrine for peace support operations. Pretoria: Institute for defence policy.

Porteous, T. 2004. Resolving African conflicts. Crimes of war project: Wars in Africa.

Ram, S and J. Shreesh Juyal. 1999. Peacekeeping in the former Yugoslavia: from the Dayton accord to Kosovo. New York: UNITAR POCI.

Ramsbotham, A., M.S. Bah and F. Calder. 2005. The implementation of the joint Africa/G8 plan to enhance African capabilities to undertake peace support operations: survey of current G8 and African activities and potential areas for further collaboration. London: Chatham house.

Robbins, S.P. 2001. Organisational behaviour, Ed 9. New York: Prentice Hall.

Roberts, A. 1996. The crisis in UN peacekeeping. In: C.

Reid, M.A., H. Barrington and J. Kennedy. 1992. Training interventions: managing employee development. London: Institute of Personnel Management.

Rothwell, W.J. and H.C. Kazanas. 1992. Mastering the instructional design process. San Francisco: Jossey-Bass.

Rothwell, W.J. and H.C. Kazanas. 1998. Mastering the instructional design process: A systematic process, Ed 2. San Francisco: Jossey-Bass.

Rothwell, W.J. and H.H. Stredi. 1992. The ASTD reference guide to professional human resource development roles and competencies, Ed 2. Massachusetts: HRD Press.

Schneider. B, S.D. Asworth, A.C. Higgs, and L. Carr. 1996. Design, validity, and use of strategically focussed employee attitude surveys. Personnel psychology journal, 49. p.695-705.

Seels, B.B. 1995. Instructional design fundamentals. Englewood Cliffs: Educational Technology Publication.

Shaw, M and J. Cilliers. 1995. South Africa and peacekeeping in Africa, Volume 1. Halfway House: Institute for Defence Policy.

Sheal, P. 1994. Staff training courses. London: Kogan Page.

Slavin, R.E. 1990. Research on cooperative learning: consensus and controversy. Educational Leadership, 47(4), 52-54.

Smith, P.L. and T.J. Ragan. 1999. Instructional design. Upper Saddle River, NJ: Merrill/Prentice Hall.

Spady, W.G. 1994. Outcome-based education: critical issues and answers. Arlington: American Association of School of Administrators.

South Africa. 1996. Constitution of the Republic of South Africa, Act 108 of 1996. Pretoria: Government printer.

South Africa. 1998. White paper on participation in international peacekeeping operations. Pretoria: 1 Military Printing Regiment.

South Africa. 1998. Skills Development Act, Act 97 of 1998. 20 Oct. Pretoria: Government printer.

South Africa. 1995. South African Qualifications Authority Act, Act 58 of 1995. 4 Oct. Pretoria: Government printer.

South Africa. 1998. White paper on South African participation in international peace missions. Pretoria: Government printer.

South African Ministry of Defence. 2001. Dodi CCS No 1/2001: Military Strategy. Pretoria: Government printer.

South African National Defence Force College of Educational Technology (SANDF COLET). 2003a. Design and conduct research (NQF level 5). Pretoria: SANDF COLET.

South African National Defence Force College of Educational Technology. 2003b. Plan a learning programme. Pretoria: SANDF COLET.

South African National Defence Force College of Educational Technology. 2004a. Prepare learning aids. Pretoria: SANDF COLET.

South African National Defence Force College of Educational Technology. 2004b. Plan and conduct of an assessment. Pretoria: SANDF COLET.

South African National Defence Force College of Educational Technology. 2006a. Outcomes-based education and training. Pretoria: SANDF COLET.

South African National Defence Force College of Educational Technology. 2006b. ETD programme: assessment guide. Pretoria: SANDF COLET.

South African National Defence Force National War College. Nd. Elements of a geo-political study. Pretoria: SA National War College Reader SG05S.

South African National Defence Force. 2005. JWP 106 part 2: Peace support operations. Pretoria: Department of Defence.

South African Department of Defence. 1998. Defence review (0-9584190-8-6). Pretoria: 1 Military Printing Regiment.

South African Department of Defence. 1996. White paper on Defence (0-9584190-8-6). Pretoria: 1 Military Printing Regiment.

South African Department of Defence. 2001. Department of defence human resource strategy 2010. Pretoria: 1 Military Printing Regiment.

South African Qualifications Authority. 2001. Criteria and guidelines for assessment of NQF registered unit standards and qualifications: policy document. Pretoria. SAQA.

SPSS. 1999. SPSS for windows, ver. 10.0.5. Cape Town: SPSS Inc.

Steyn, P. 1997. South Africa and peace support operations; limitations, options, and challenges. Conference on Contemporary Peace Support Operations. Pretoria, 5 Nov.

Studer, M. 2001. The ICRC and civil-military relations in armed conflict. IRRC June, Vol. 83 No. 842.

Thiart G. 1997. Africa's eagle of hope has landed. Pretoria: SALUT, vol. 4, no.6, p. 12.

Tovey, M. 1997. Training in Australia. Sydney: Prentice Hall Australia.

Tsedu, T. 2002. Marching away from home and family. Saturday Star, 28 Dec 02, p.6.

Tracy, W.R. 1984. Designing training and development systems. New York: Amacon.

Trench, A. 1998. Can we get it up for war? Sunday Times, 11 Jan 1998, p.15.

Training for Peace (TFP). 2004. Peace support operations, training for peace in Southern Africa programme. http://www.trainingforpeace.org/themes/supp/htm.

UK Ministry of Defence. 2004. Peace support operations; joint warfare publication 3-50 (JWP 3-50). United Kingdom.

United Nations. 2003. Handbook on UN multidimensional peacekeeping operations. http://pbpu.inlb.org/pbpu/handbook.

United Nations Department of Peacekeeping Operations (DPKO). 1995. General guidelines for peacekeeping operations (UN/210/TC/GG95). New York: International Training Centre of the ILO.

United Nations Department of Peacekeeping Operations (DPKO). 2003. Standardized Generic Training Module's (SGTM) 1A – Introduction to the UN system. New York: International Training Centre of the ILO.

United Nations Department of Peacekeeping Operations (DPKO). 2003. Standardized Generic Training Module's (SGTM) 1B - UN peacekeeping operations. New York: International Training Centre of the ILO.

United Nations Department of Peacekeeping Operations (DPKO). 2003. Standardized Generic Training Module's (SGTM) 06 – Personal security awareness. New York: International Training Centre of the ILO.

United Nations Department of Peacekeeping Operations (DPKO). 2003. Standardized Generic Training Module's (SGTM) 9 – UN Humanitarian Assistance. New York: International Training Centre of the ILO.

United Nations Department of Peacekeeping Operations (DPKO). 2003. Standardized Generic Training Module's (SGTM) 10 – UN civil-military coordination. New York: International Training Centre of the ILO.

United Nations Department of Peacekeeping Operations (DPKO). 2003. Standardized Generic Training Module's (SGTM) 15 – UN logistics. New York: International Training Centre of the ILO.

UNISA. 2003. Co-operative education policy. Florida: UNISA

USA Department of Defence. 1995. Joint Publication 3-07: Joint Doctrine for Military Operations other that War. United States: Department of Defence.

Van der Westhuizen, P.C. 1998. Effective educational management. Pretoria: Kagiso.

Van der Westhuizen, J.P.C. 1998. The changing context of education, training and development. Pretoria: SANDF Bulletin for Educational Technology. Vol 22 No 2, p.29.

Van der Westhuizen, C. 2005. International politics. Pretoria: Institute for Global Dialogue, 9 Feb 2005.

Van Niekerk, R.1991a. Ed Tech 2: PF Offs: Study Collection D: The process of instructional design. Pretoria: SANDF COLET.

Van Niekerk, R.1991b. Ed Tech 2: PF Offs: Study Collection H: Practical work assignment. Pretoria: SANDF COLET.

Van der Spuy, M., P.J. Cronje and S. Breytenbach. 2005. Department of Defence Instruction (DODI), Trg No 00006/2003 (2nd Ed): Management of learner assessment by providers in the DOD. Pretoria.

Van der Walt, A. 2005. What is educational technology? Pretoria: SANDF COLET.

Van Dyk, P.S., P.S. Nel, and Van Z Loedolff. 1992. Training management: a multidisciplinary approach to human resource development in Southern Africa. Cape Town: Oxford.

Van Dyk, P.S., P.S. Nel, Van Z Loedolff, and G.D. Haasbroek. 2001. Training management: a multidisciplinary approach to human resource development in Southern Africa, Ed 3. Cape Town: Oxford.

Welman J. C., Kruger S. J. 1999. Research methodology for the business and administrative sciences. Halfway house: Thomson publishing.

Weinstein, M.A. 2004. An era of instability in world politics. http://www.pinr.com/bios.php.

Walkinshaw, G.C. 1992. "Wetenskaplike benadering tot ontwerp van kursusse". SAW Bulletin vir Opvoedkundige Tegnologie, 16(2): 13 -19.

Wilkinson, P. R. 1998. Sharpening the weapons of peace; the development of a common military doctrine for peace support operations. UK British Army Review, April Ed.

Wilkinson, P.R. and R.J. Rinaldo. 1996. Principles for the conduct of peace support operations. New York: UNITAR POCI.

Wills, M. 1998. Managing the training process: putting the principles into practice. Hampshire: Gower.

Wilson, J.B. 1995. Mapping a winning training approach: a practical guide to choosing the right training materials. Irvine, California: Richard Chang.

Woodhouse. T and T. Duffey. 2000. Peacekeeping and international conflict resolution. New York: UNITAR POCI.

Wolfe, A. 2005. The increasing importance of African oil. http://www.pinr.com

Wolmarans, I.S. and J.J. Eksteen. 1987. "Behoeftebepaling: besin voor jy begin". Johannesgurg: Gutengerg

Zemke, R. 1999. Training isn't education lite. Training: the human side of business: 8-10.

Lightning Source UK Ltd.
Milton Keynes UK
UKOW050449131011

180253UK00001B/116/P